TEACHER'S PET PUBLICATIONS

PUZZLE PACK
for
The Call of the Wild
based on the book by
Jack London

Written by
William T. Collins

© 2005 Teacher's Pet Publications
All Rights Reserved

The materials in this packet are copyrighted
by Teacher's Pet Publications, Inc.

These pages may be duplicated by the purchaser
for use in the purchaser's own classroom.

Copying any of these materials and distributing them
for any other purpose is a violation of the copyright laws.

© 2005 Teacher's Pet Publications, Inc.
www.tpet.com

INTRODUCTION
If you already own the LitPlan for this title, this Puzzle Pack will refresh your Unit Resource Materials and Vocabulary Resource Materials sections plus give you additional materials you can substitute into the tests. If you do not already have a complete LitPlan, these pages will give you some supplemental materials to use with your own plan. There are two main groups of materials: one set for unit words (such as characters' names, symbols, places, etc.) and one set for vocabulary words associated with the book.

WORD LIST
There is a word list for both the unit words and the vocabulary words. These lists show you which words are being used in the materials and the clues or definitions being used for those words. You may want to give students a word list with clues/definitions to help them, or you may want students to only have a word list (without clues/definitions) if you want them to work a little harder. Both are available for duplication. The word lists can also be your "calling key" for the bingo games.

FILL IN THE BLANK AND MATCHING
There are 4 each of the fill in the blank and matching worksheets for both the unit and vocabulary words. These pages can be used either as extra worksheets for students or as objective parts of a unit test. They can be done individually if students need extra help or as a whole class activity to review the material covered.

MAGIC SQUARES
The magic squares not only reinforce the material covered but also work on reasoning and math skills. Many teachers have told us that their students really enjoy doing these!

WORD SEARCH PUZZLES
The word search words go in all directions, as indicated on your answer keys. Two of the word search puzzles have the clues listed rather than the words. This makes the puzzle a little more difficult, but it reinforces the material better. Two word search puzzles have words only for students who find the clue puzzles too difficult.

CROSSWORD PUZZLES
Both unit and vocabulary word sections have 4 crossword puzzles.

BINGO CARDS
There are 32 individual bingo cards for the unit words and 32 individual bingo cards for the vocabulary words. You can use your word list as a "call list," calling the words at random and marking them off of your list as you go, or you could use the flash cards by cutting them apart and drawing the words at random from a hat (or box or whatever). To make a better review, you might ask for the definition and spelling of each word as you call it out–or you could call out the definitions and have students tell you the words they need to look for on the puzzle.

JUGGLE LETTERS
The vocabulary juggle letter game is intended to help students learn the spellings of the words. One sheet has the definitions listed on it as an extra help for students who need it or to reinforce the definitions if you choose to do so.

FLASH CARDS
We've included a set of vocabulary flash cards you can duplicate, cut, and fold for your students. Some teachers make a few sets for general use by the class; others make a set for each student. Some teachers duplicate them for each student and have the students cut & fold their own. You can cut out just the words and put them in a hat, have each student pick out one word and write the definition and a sentence for that word. Students then swap words and papers, with the next student adding a sentence of his own under the last one. You can have students swap as many times as you like. Each time the student will read the sentences written prior to his own and then add a sentence. You can cut out the words and definitions separately and play "I Have; Who Has?" Each student in the room draws a word and definition. The first student says, "I have (the name of the word). Who has the definition?" The student with the definition reads it then says, "I have (the name of the vocabulary word she has). Who has the definition?" The round continues until all words and definitions have been given.

The Call of the Wild Word List

No.	Word	Clue/Definition
1.	ALL	Not part of everyone
2.	ATE	Past tense of eat
3.	BASE	Camp from which one goes out
4.	BURTON	Black _____; Buck killed him for hitting Thornton
5.	CHARLES	Buck's ignorant owner from the south
6.	CLUB	The man in the read sweater had one
7.	COLD	Chilly; opposite of hot
8.	CURLY	Spitz killed this Newfoundland
9.	DIE	Opposite of live
10.	DOG	Buck, for example
11.	EAR	Hearing organ
12.	FANG	The Law Buck learned: Club and ___
13.	FIGHT	Buck and Spitz did this
14.	FRANCOIS	Worked with Perrault
15.	GHOST	What Indians called Buck: ___ Dog
16.	GOLD	Yellow metal discovered in the North
17.	HAL	Mercedes' brother
18.	HARNESS	It holds dogs together and to the sled
19.	HIT	Black Burton _____ John Thornton
20.	HO	Stop - Command
21.	HOWL	Wolves _____ at the moon
22.	ICE	Frozen water
23.	JUDGE	Mr. Miller's official title
24.	LOYALTY	Traits of dogs; _____ to their owners
25.	MAIL	Job of the Scott half-breed: ___ Train
26.	MANUEL	Gardener's helper; sold Buck
27.	MERCEDES	Charles's wife
28.	MILLER	Buck's California owner
29.	MOOSE	Large animal Buck killed
30.	MUSH	Go - Command
31.	NIG	Dog at John's camp
32.	OBRIEN	Thornton's friend
33.	PART	Buck had to _____ with many owners; leave
34.	PAWS	Dog's feet
35.	PERRAULT	He worked with Francois
36.	PRIDE	To take _____ in one's work
37.	RED	Color of blood and sweater
38.	RIVER	Charles, Hal & Mercedes are killed trying to cross one
39.	SLED	Thing the dogs pulled
40.	SNOW	Dogs have to work hard when it is deep
41.	SOLLEKS	Name means angry one
42.	SOUTH	Opposite of North
43.	SPITZ	Buck killed this leader-dog
44.	SURVIVAL	_____ of the fittest
45.	SWEATER	Man in the red _____
46.	TEAM	Dogs worked together
47.	THIEF	One who steals
48.	THORNTON	Buck's last master-friend
49.	TORN	Ripped
50.	TURN	Go right or left
51.	USE	You _____ the whip to keep order

The Call of the Wild Word List

No.	Word	Clue/Definition
52.	WOLF	Animal(s) Buck met in Wilderness
53.	WOODS	Where John and Buck went
54.	YEEHATS	Indian tribe

The Call of the Wild Fill In The Blanks 1

_____   1. You _____ the whip to keep order

_____   2. Large animal Buck killed

_____   3. Traits of dogs; _____ to their owners

_____   4. It holds dogs together and to the sled

_____   5. Dogs worked together

_____   6. One who steals

_____   7. Stop - Command

_____   8. Thornton's friend

_____   9. Color of blood and sweater

_____   10. Not part of everyone

_____   11. Opposite of live

_____   12. Spitz killed this Newfoundland

_____   13. Buck's ignorant owner from the south

_____   14. The man in the read sweater had one

_____   15. Gardener's helper; sold Buck

_____   16. Buck's California owner

_____   17. Chilly; opposite of hot

_____   18. Mercedes' brother

_____   19. Charles, Hal & Mercedes are killed trying to cross one

_____   20. Animal(s) Buck met in Wilderness

The Call of the Wild Fill In The Blanks 1 Answer Key

USE	1. You _____ the whip to keep order
MOOSE	2. Large animal Buck killed
LOYALTY	3. Traits of dogs; _____ to their owners
HARNESS	4. It holds dogs together and to the sled
TEAM	5. Dogs worked together
THIEF	6. One who steals
HO	7. Stop - Command
OBRIEN	8. Thornton's friend
RED	9. Color of blood and sweater
ALL	10. Not part of everyone
DIE	11. Opposite of live
CURLY	12. Spitz killed this Newfoundland
CHARLES	13. Buck's ignorant owner from the south
CLUB	14. The man in the read sweater had one
MANUEL	15. Gardener's helper; sold Buck
MILLER	16. Buck's California owner
COLD	17. Chilly; opposite of hot
HAL	18. Mercedes' brother
RIVER	19. Charles, Hal & Mercedes are killed trying to cross one
WOLF	20. Animal(s) Buck met in Wilderness

The Call of the Wild Fill In The Blanks 2

_____ 1. Black _____; Buck killed him for hitting Thornton
_____ 2. Chilly; opposite of hot
_____ 3. Name means angry one
_____ 4. Buck, for example
_____ 5. Stop - Command
_____ 6. Thornton's friend
_____ 7. Worked with Perrault
_____ 8. Thing the dogs pulled
_____ 9. Dogs have to work hard when it is deep
_____ 10. You _____ the whip to keep order
_____ 11. Buck killed this leader-dog
_____ 12. Indian tribe
_____ 13. Opposite of North
_____ 14. Hearing organ
_____ 15. Large animal Buck killed
_____ 16. Go - Command
_____ 17. Dog's feet
_____ 18. Color of blood and sweater
_____ 19. Opposite of live
_____ 20. Job of the Scott half-breed: ___ Train

The Call of the Wild Fill In The Blanks 2 Answer Key

BURTON	1. Black _____; Buck killed him for hitting Thornton
COLD	2. Chilly; opposite of hot
SOLLEKS	3. Name means angry one
DOG	4. Buck, for example
HO	5. Stop - Command
OBRIEN	6. Thornton's friend
FRANCOIS	7. Worked with Perrault
SLED	8. Thing the dogs pulled
SNOW	9. Dogs have to work hard when it is deep
USE	10. You _____ the whip to keep order
SPITZ	11. Buck killed this leader-dog
YEEHATS	12. Indian tribe
SOUTH	13. Opposite of North
EAR	14. Hearing organ
MOOSE	15. Large animal Buck killed
MUSH	16. Go - Command
PAWS	17. Dog's feet
RED	18. Color of blood and sweater
DIE	19. Opposite of live
MAIL	20. Job of the Scott half-breed: ___ Train

The Call of the Wild Fill In The Blanks 3

_____

1. Man in the red _____
2. Camp from which one goes out
3. Chilly; opposite of hot
4. Buck and Spitz did this
5. Hearing organ
6. Thornton's friend
7. Dogs have to work hard when it is deep
8. Thing the dogs pulled
9. Buck's last master-friend
10. The man in the read sweater had one
11. Wolves _____ at the moon
12. Dog's feet
13. Past tense of eat
14. Buck's California owner
15. What Indians called Buck: ___ Dog
16. Name means angry one
17. He worked with Francois
18. Ripped
19. You _____ the whip to keep order
20. Buck's ignorant owner from the south

The Call of the Wild Fill In The Blanks 3 Answer Key

SWEATER	1. Man in the red _____
BASE	2. Camp from which one goes out
COLD	3. Chilly; opposite of hot
FIGHT	4. Buck and Spitz did this
EAR	5. Hearing organ
OBRIEN	6. Thornton's friend
SNOW	7. Dogs have to work hard when it is deep
SLED	8. Thing the dogs pulled
THORNTON	9. Buck's last master-friend
CLUB	10. The man in the read sweater had one
HOWL	11. Wolves _____ at the moon
PAWS	12. Dog's feet
ATE	13. Past tense of eat
MILLER	14. Buck's California owner
GHOST	15. What Indians called Buck: ___ Dog
SOLLEKS	16. Name means angry one
PERRAULT	17. He worked with Francois
TORN	18. Ripped
USE	19. You _____ the whip to keep order
CHARLES	20. Buck's ignorant owner from the south

The Call of the Wild Fill In The Blanks 4

_____ 1. Thornton's friend

_____ 2. Buck's last master-friend

_____ 3. Stop - Command

_____ 4. Buck killed this leader-dog

_____ 5. Where John and Buck went

_____ 6. Large animal Buck killed

_____ 7. Go right or left

_____ 8. Animal(s) Buck met in Wilderness

_____ 9. He worked with Francois

_____ 10. Color of blood and sweater

_____ 11. Buck had to _____ with many owners; leave

_____ 12. Not part of everyone

_____ 13. Job of the Scott half-breed: ___ Train

_____ 14. Past tense of eat

_____ 15. Wolves _____ at the moon

_____ 16. One who steals

_____ 17. It holds dogs together and to the sled

_____ 18. Mr. Miller's official title

_____ 19. Opposite of live

_____ 20. Frozen water

The Call of the Wild Fill In The Blanks 4 Answer Key

OBRIEN	1. Thornton's friend
THORNTON	2. Buck's last master-friend
HO	3. Stop - Command
SPITZ	4. Buck killed this leader-dog
WOODS	5. Where John and Buck went
MOOSE	6. Large animal Buck killed
TURN	7. Go right or left
WOLF	8. Animal(s) Buck met in Wilderness
PERRAULT	9. He worked with Francois
RED	10. Color of blood and sweater
PART	11. Buck had to _____ with many owners; leave
ALL	12. Not part of everyone
MAIL	13. Job of the Scott half-breed: ___ Train
ATE	14. Past tense of eat
HOWL	15. Wolves _____ at the moon
THIEF	16. One who steals
HARNESS	17. It holds dogs together and to the sled
JUDGE	18. Mr. Miller's official title
DIE	19. Opposite of live
ICE	20. Frozen water

The Call of the Wild Matching 1

___ 1. CHARLES   A. Spitz killed this Newfoundland
___ 2. TORN   B. Dogs have to work hard when it is deep
___ 3. THIEF   C. Indian tribe
___ 4. CURLY   D. Ripped
___ 5. MAIL   E. Opposite of live
___ 6. MUSH   F. Job of the Scott half-breed: ___ Train
___ 7. WOLF   G. Where John and Buck went
___ 8. WOODS   H. Black _____; Buck killed him for hitting Thornton
___ 9. HARNESS   I. One who steals
___10. NIG   J. Dogs worked together
___11. YEEHATS   K. You _____ the whip to keep order
___12. THORNTON   L. It holds dogs together and to the sled
___13. GOLD   M. Go right or left
___14. RIVER   N. Hearing organ
___15. TURN   O. Charles, Hal & Mercedes are killed trying to cross one
___16. TEAM   P. Dog at John's camp
___17. SOLLEKS   Q. The man in the read sweater had one
___18. EAR   R. Yellow metal discovered in the North
___19. ICE   S. Buck's ignorant owner from the south
___20. DIE   T. Animal(s) Buck met in Wilderness
___21. USE   U. Frozen water
___22. CLUB   V. Go - Command
___23. SNOW   W. Buck's last master-friend
___24. BURTON   X. Large animal Buck killed
___25. MOOSE   Y. Name means angry one

The Call of the Wild Matching 1 Answer Key

S - 1. CHARLES   A. Spitz killed this Newfoundland
D - 2. TORN   B. Dogs have to work hard when it is deep
I - 3. THIEF   C. Indian tribe
A - 4. CURLY   D. Ripped
F - 5. MAIL   E. Opposite of live
V - 6. MUSH   F. Job of the Scott half-breed: ___ Train
T - 7. WOLF   G. Where John and Buck went
G - 8. WOODS   H. Black _____; Buck killed him for hitting Thornton
L - 9. HARNESS   I. One who steals
P - 10. NIG   J. Dogs worked together
C - 11. YEEHATS   K. You _____ the whip to keep order
W - 12. THORNTON   L. It holds dogs together and to the sled
R - 13. GOLD   M. Go right or left
O - 14. RIVER   N. Hearing organ
M - 15. TURN   O. Charles, Hal & Mercedes are killed trying to cross one
J - 16. TEAM   P. Dog at John's camp
Y - 17. SOLLEKS   Q. The man in the read sweater had one
N - 18. EAR   R. Yellow metal discovered in the North
U - 19. ICE   S. Buck's ignorant owner from the south
E - 20. DIE   T. Animal(s) Buck met in Wilderness
K - 21. USE   U. Frozen water
Q - 22. CLUB   V. Go - Command
B - 23. SNOW   W. Buck's last master-friend
H - 24. BURTON   X. Large animal Buck killed
X - 25. MOOSE   Y. Name means angry one

The Call of the Wild Matching 2

___ 1. MUSH   A. Buck and Spitz did this
___ 2. HAL   B. Frozen water
___ 3. MERCEDES   C. Thing the dogs pulled
___ 4. WOLF   D. _____ of the fittest
___ 5. DOG   E. Traits of dogs; _____ to their owners
___ 6. RIVER   F. Dogs have to work hard when it is deep
___ 7. HARNESS   G. Hearing organ
___ 8. SLED   H. Charles's wife
___ 9. MANUEL   I. Animal(s) Buck met in Wilderness
___10. SOUTH   J. To take _____ in one's work
___11. SURVIVAL   K. Gardener's helper; sold Buck
___12. YEEHATS   L. Name means angry one
___13. PERRAULT   M. Man in the red _____
___14. SOLLEKS   N. Buck, for example
___15. FANG   O. Go - Command
___16. FIGHT   P. Wolves _____ at the moon
___17. ICE   Q. Mercedes' brother
___18. COLD   R. Not part of everyone
___19. EAR   S. He worked with Francois
___20. ALL   T. Indian tribe
___21. SNOW   U. Charles, Hal & Mercedes are killed trying to cross one
___22. SWEATER   V. The Law Buck learned: Club and ___
___23. HOWL   W. It holds dogs together and to the sled
___24. LOYALTY   X. Opposite of North
___25. PRIDE   Y. Chilly; opposite of hot

The Call of the Wild Matching 2 Answer Key

- O - 1. MUSH
- Q - 2. HAL
- H - 3. MERCEDES
- I - 4. WOLF
- N - 5. DOG
- U - 6. RIVER
- W - 7. HARNESS
- C - 8. SLED
- K - 9. MANUEL
- X - 10. SOUTH
- D - 11. SURVIVAL
- T - 12. YEEHATS
- S - 13. PERRAULT
- L - 14. SOLLEKS
- V - 15. FANG
- A - 16. FIGHT
- B - 17. ICE
- Y - 18. COLD
- G - 19. EAR
- R - 20. ALL
- F - 21. SNOW
- M - 22. SWEATER
- P - 23. HOWL
- E - 24. LOYALTY
- J - 25. PRIDE

A. Buck and Spitz did this
B. Frozen water
C. Thing the dogs pulled
D. _____ of the fittest
E. Traits of dogs; _____ to their owners
F. Dogs have to work hard when it is deep
G. Hearing organ
H. Charles's wife
I. Animal(s) Buck met in Wilderness
J. To take _____ in one's work
K. Gardener's helper; sold Buck
L. Name means angry one
M. Man in the red _____
N. Buck, for example
O. Go - Command
P. Wolves _____ at the moon
Q. Mercedes' brother
R. Not part of everyone
S. He worked with Francois
T. Indian tribe
U. Charles, Hal & Mercedes are killed trying to cross one
V. The Law Buck learned: Club and ___
W. It holds dogs together and to the sled
X. Opposite of North
Y. Chilly; opposite of hot

The Call of the Wild Matching 3

___ 1. HOWL   A. Ripped
___ 2. OBRIEN   B. Opposite of North
___ 3. PRIDE   C. Charles, Hal & Mercedes are killed trying to cross one
___ 4. RED   D. Thornton's friend
___ 5. MILLER   E. One who steals
___ 6. LOYALTY   F. Hearing organ
___ 7. SOUTH   G. Buck's California owner
___ 8. WOODS   H. Buck had to _____ with many owners; leave
___ 9. THIEF   I. Worked with Perrault
___10. FIGHT   J. Buck, for example
___11. DOG   K. The man in the read sweater had one
___12. PERRAULT   L. Mercedes' brother
___13. NIG   M. Traits of dogs; _____ to their owners
___14. SPITZ   N. Buck killed this leader-dog
___15. EAR   O. Dog at John's camp
___16. BASE   P. He worked with Francois
___17. JUDGE   Q. Stop - Command
___18. HO   R. Wolves _____ at the moon
___19. FRANCOIS   S. Mr. Miller's official title
___20. MUSH   T. Where John and Buck went
___21. RIVER   U. To take _____ in one's work
___22. HAL   V. Go - Command
___23. CLUB   W. Buck and Spitz did this
___24. PART   X. Camp from which one goes out
___25. TORN   Y. Color of blood and sweater

The Call of the Wild Matching 3 Answer Key

R - 1. HOWL	A.	Ripped
D - 2. OBRIEN	B.	Opposite of North
U - 3. PRIDE	C.	Charles, Hal & Mercedes are killed trying to cross one
Y - 4. RED	D.	Thornton's friend
G - 5. MILLER	E.	One who steals
M - 6. LOYALTY	F.	Hearing organ
B - 7. SOUTH	G.	Buck's California owner
T - 8. WOODS	H.	Buck had to _____ with many owners; leave
E - 9. THIEF	I.	Worked with Perrault
W - 10. FIGHT	J.	Buck, for example
J - 11. DOG	K.	The man in the read sweater had one
P - 12. PERRAULT	L.	Mercedes' brother
O - 13. NIG	M.	Traits of dogs; _____ to their owners
N - 14. SPITZ	N.	Buck killed this leader-dog
F - 15. EAR	O.	Dog at John's camp
X - 16. BASE	P.	He worked with Francois
S - 17. JUDGE	Q.	Stop - Command
Q - 18. HO	R.	Wolves _____ at the moon
I - 19. FRANCOIS	S.	Mr. Miller's official title
V - 20. MUSH	T.	Where John and Buck went
C - 21. RIVER	U.	To take _____ in one's work
L - 22. HAL	V.	Go - Command
K - 23. CLUB	W.	Buck and Spitz did this
H - 24. PART	X.	Camp from which one goes out
A - 25. TORN	Y.	Color of blood and sweater

The Call of the Wild Matching 4

___ 1. WOLF   A. Buck had to _____ with many owners; leave
___ 2. MOOSE   B. Color of blood and sweater
___ 3. BASE   C. You _____ the whip to keep order
___ 4. TURN   D. Thing the dogs pulled
___ 5. HO   E. Buck and Spitz did this
___ 6. SLED   F. Dogs worked together
___ 7. HARNESS   G. Go right or left
___ 8. YEEHATS   H. It holds dogs together and to the sled
___ 9. BURTON   I. Where John and Buck went
___10. EAR   J. Hearing organ
___11. PERRAULT   K. Large animal Buck killed
___12. ICE   L. Past tense of eat
___13. USE   M. Black Burton _____ John Thornton
___14. ATE   N. The Law Buck learned: Club and ___
___15. COLD   O. Chilly; opposite of hot
___16. HIT   P. Charles's wife
___17. MANUEL   Q. Black _____; Buck killed him for hitting Thornton
___18. RED   R. Frozen water
___19. MAIL   S. He worked with Francois
___20. PART   T. Camp from which one goes out
___21. FIGHT   U. Indian tribe
___22. TEAM   V. Animal(s) Buck met in Wilderness
___23. MERCEDES   W. Job of the Scott half-breed: ___ Train
___24. WOODS   X. Stop - Command
___25. FANG   Y. Gardener's helper; sold Buck

The Call of the Wild Matching 4 Answer Key

V - 1.	WOLF	A. Buck had to _____ with many owners; leave
K - 2.	MOOSE	B. Color of blood and sweater
T - 3.	BASE	C. You _____ the whip to keep order
G - 4.	TURN	D. Thing the dogs pulled
X - 5.	HO	E. Buck and Spitz did this
D - 6.	SLED	F. Dogs worked together
H - 7.	HARNESS	G. Go right or left
U - 8.	YEEHATS	H. It holds dogs together and to the sled
Q - 9.	BURTON	I. Where John and Buck went
J - 10.	EAR	J. Hearing organ
S - 11.	PERRAULT	K. Large animal Buck killed
R - 12.	ICE	L. Past tense of eat
C - 13.	USE	M. Black Burton _____ John Thornton
L - 14.	ATE	N. The Law Buck learned: Club and ___
O - 15.	COLD	O. Chilly; opposite of hot
M - 16.	HIT	P. Charles's wife
Y - 17.	MANUEL	Q. Black _____; Buck killed him for hitting Thornton
B - 18.	RED	R. Frozen water
W - 19.	MAIL	S. He worked with Francois
A - 20.	PART	T. Camp from which one goes out
E - 21.	FIGHT	U. Indian tribe
F - 22.	TEAM	V. Animal(s) Buck met in Wilderness
P - 23.	MERCEDES	W. Job of the Scott half-breed: ___ Train
I - 24.	WOODS	X. Stop - Command
N - 25.	FANG	Y. Gardener's helper; sold Buck

The Call of the Wild Magic Squares 1

Match the definition with the vocabulary word. Put your answers in the magic squares below. When your answers are correct, all columns and rows will add to the same number.

A. FIGHT
B. THIEF
C. MAIL
D. HARNESS
E. LOYALTY
F. SOUTH
G. CLUB
H. HO
I. THORNTON
J. MILLER
K. TURN
L. JUDGE
M. USE
N. TORN
O. HIT
P. COLD

1. Job of the Scott half-breed: ___ Train
2. Buck's California owner
3. Opposite of North
4. Black Burton _____ John Thornton
5. Chilly; opposite of hot
6. Traits of dogs; _____ to their owners
7. Buck's last master-friend
8. It holds dogs together and to the sled
9. You _____ the whip to keep order
10. Stop - Command
11. Mr. Miller's official title
12. Buck and Spitz did this
13. One who steals
14. Go right or left
15. The man in the read sweater had one
16. Ripped

A=	B=	C=	D=
E=	F=	G=	H=
I=	J=	K=	L=
M=	N=	O=	P=

The Call of the Wild Magic Squares 1 Answer Key

Match the definition with the vocabulary word. Put your answers in the magic squares below. When your answers are correct, all columns and rows will add to the same number.

A. FIGHT
B. THIEF
C. MAIL
D. HARNESS
E. LOYALTY
F. SOUTH
G. CLUB
H. HO
I. THORNTON
J. MILLER
K. TURN
L. JUDGE
M. USE
N. TORN
O. HIT
P. COLD

1. Job of the Scott half-breed: ___ Train
2. Buck's California owner
3. Opposite of North
4. Black Burton _____ John Thornton
5. Chilly; opposite of hot
6. Traits of dogs; _____ to their owners
7. Buck's last master-friend
8. It holds dogs together and to the sled
9. You _____ the whip to keep order
10. Stop - Command
11. Mr. Miller's official title
12. Buck and Spitz did this
13. One who steals
14. Go right or left
15. The man in the read sweater had one
16. Ripped

A=12	B=13	C=1	D=8
E=6	F=3	G=15	H=10
I=7	J=2	K=14	L=11
M=9	N=16	O=4	P=5

The Call of the Wild Magic Squares 2

Match the definition with the vocabulary word. Put your answers in the magic squares below. When your answers are correct, all columns and rows will add to the same number.

A. JUDGE   E. GOLD   I. DIE   M. TURN
B. THORNTON F. WOLF   J. PART   N. COLD
C. YEEHATS   G. FIGHT   K. MANUEL   O. SLED
D. LOYALTY   H. PRIDE   L. GHOST   P. BURTON

1. Mr. Miller's official title
2. Chilly; opposite of hot
3. Buck had to _____ with many owners; leave
4. Yellow metal discovered in the North
5. Buck and Spitz did this
6. What Indians called Buck: ___ Dog
7. Black _____; Buck killed him for hitting Thornton
8. Indian tribe
9. Thing the dogs pulled
10. Traits of dogs; _____ to their owners
11. To take _____ in one's work
12. Gardener's helper; sold Buck
13. Opposite of live
14. Animal(s) Buck met in Wilderness
15. Buck's last master-friend
16. Go right or left

A=	B=	C=	D=
E=	F=	G=	H=
I=	J=	K=	L=
M=	N=	O=	P=

The Call of the Wild Magic Squares 2 Answer Key

Match the definition with the vocabulary word. Put your answers in the magic squares below. When your answers are correct, all columns and rows will add to the same number.

A. JUDGE
B. THORNTON
C. YEEHATS
D. LOYALTY
E. GOLD
F. WOLF
G. FIGHT
H. PRIDE
I. DIE
J. PART
K. MANUEL
L. GHOST
M. TURN
N. COLD
O. SLED
P. BURTON

1. Mr. Miller's official title
2. Chilly; opposite of hot
3. Buck had to _____ with many owners; leave
4. Yellow metal discovered in the North
5. Buck and Spitz did this
6. What Indians called Buck: ___ Dog
7. Black _____; Buck killed him for hitting Thornton
8. Indian tribe
9. Thing the dogs pulled
10. Traits of dogs; _____ to their owners
11. To take _____ in one's work
12. Gardener's helper; sold Buck
13. Opposite of live
14. Animal(s) Buck met in Wilderness
15. Buck's last master-friend
16. Go right or left

A=1	B=15	C=8	D=10
E=4	F=14	G=5	H=11
I=13	J=3	K=12	L=6
M=16	N=2	O=9	P=7

The Call of the Wild Magic Squares 3

Match the definition with the vocabulary word. Put your answers in the magic squares below. When your answers are correct, all columns and rows will add to the same number.

A. RED   E. GOLD   I. SNOW   M. HAL
B. LOYALTY   F. USE   J. JUDGE   N. MANUEL
C. SLED   G. DIE   K. THORNTON   O. EAR
D. ALL   H. NIG   L. CHARLES   P. DOG

1. Hearing organ
2. Mr. Miller's official title
3. Dog at John's camp
4. Color of blood and sweater
5. Not part of everyone
6. Yellow metal discovered in the North
7. Buck's last master-friend
8. Gardener's helper; sold Buck
9. You _____ the whip to keep order
10. Thing the dogs pulled
11. Mercedes' brother
12. Buck's ignorant owner from the south
13. Dogs have to work hard when it is deep
14. Buck, for example
15. Traits of dogs; _____ to their owners
16. Opposite of live

A=	B=	C=	D=
E=	F=	G=	H=
I=	J=	K=	L=
M=	N=	O=	P=

The Call of the Wild Magic Squares 3 Answer Key

Match the definition with the vocabulary word. Put your answers in the magic squares below. When your answers are correct, all columns and rows will add to the same number.

A. RED
B. LOYALTY
C. SLED
D. ALL
E. GOLD
F. USE
G. DIE
H. NIG
I. SNOW
J. JUDGE
K. THORNTON
L. CHARLES
M. HAL
N. MANUEL
O. EAR
P. DOG

1. Hearing organ
2. Mr. Miller's official title
3. Dog at John's camp
4. Color of blood and sweater
5. Not part of everyone
6. Yellow metal discovered in the North
7. Buck's last master-friend
8. Gardener's helper; sold Buck
9. You _____ the whip to keep order
10. Thing the dogs pulled
11. Mercedes' brother
12. Buck's ignorant owner from the south
13. Dogs have to work hard when it is deep
14. Buck, for example
15. Traits of dogs; _____ to their owners
16. Opposite of live

A=4	B=15	C=10	D=5
E=6	F=9	G=16	H=3
I=13	J=2	K=7	L=12
M=11	N=8	O=1	P=14

The Call of the Wild Magic Squares 4

Match the definition with the vocabulary word. Put your answers in the magic squares below. When your answers are correct, all columns and rows will add to the same number.

A. GOLD   E. JUDGE   I. PERRAULT   M. CLUB
B. BURTON   F. TURN   J. MOOSE   N. SOUTH
C. TORN   G. ALL   K. COLD   O. FANG
D. SURVIVAL   H. WOLF   L. THORNTON   P. BASE

1. Opposite of North
2. Not part of everyone
3. Buck's last master-friend
4. Yellow metal discovered in the North
5. Chilly; opposite of hot
6. Black _____; Buck killed him for hitting Thornton
7. The man in the read sweater had one
8. Animal(s) Buck met in Wilderness
9. Mr. Miller's official title
10. Camp from which one goes out
11. Ripped
12. Large animal Buck killed
13. _____ of the fittest
14. He worked with Francois
15. Go right or left
16. The Law Buck learned: Club and ___

A=	B=	C=	D=
E=	F=	G=	H=
I=	J=	K=	L=
M=	N=	O=	P=

The Call of the Wild Magic Squares 4 Answer Key

Match the definition with the vocabulary word. Put your answers in the magic squares below. When your answers are correct, all columns and rows will add to the same number.

A. GOLD
B. BURTON
C. TORN
D. SURVIVAL
E. JUDGE
F. TURN
G. ALL
H. WOLF
I. PERRAULT
J. MOOSE
K. COLD
L. THORNTON
M. CLUB
N. SOUTH
O. FANG
P. BASE

1. Opposite of North
2. Not part of everyone
3. Buck's last master-friend
4. Yellow metal discovered in the North
5. Chilly; opposite of hot
6. Black _____; Buck killed him for hitting Thornton
7. The man in the read sweater had one
8. Animal(s) Buck met in Wilderness
9. Mr. Miller's official title
10. Camp from which one goes out
11. Ripped
12. Large animal Buck killed
13. _____ of the fittest
14. He worked with Francois
15. Go right or left
16. The Law Buck learned: Club and ___

A=4	B=6	C=11	D=13
E=9	F=15	G=2	H=8
I=14	J=12	K=5	L=3
M=7	N=1	O=16	P=10

The Call of the Wild Word Search 1

```
M K G W T H N E S S Z S N C G S N Z V
P T X C X Q H I E Y W E R H O O B J C
M A I L S L E D G A L L O Y A L T Y Q
I U R Q W N E N P Z E R T E U B L D Z G
L P S T L C A M N U Q A E U W E R H B
L A C H R F K Q N G W H L H B K O A Z
E W K E S T E A M O P C E B O S S J N
R S M Y I U M M L B C S A T E W U N
S T S H O R D F S D I R U D R S E D R
N X X W C N S R O P R I D J F A G B
O G H O N O T R U B R E D E O I T E S
W P P O A T L H T C F V M R N G E Y T
H R W D R H U O H U R I H O L H R E Z
C X Q S F I A W J R J R B X O T W E F
S P I T Z E R L B L H A R N E S S H X
Z K Z H D F R P H Y L Y F Y X T E A Y
H X R I L N E G H P X B S K D J W T Q
S Q R G T H P L H R X M L K S Y Z S J
D P T H O R N T O N S U R V I V A L C
```

Animal(s) Buck met in Wilderness (4)
Black Burton _____ John Thornton (3)
Black _____; Buck killed him for hitting Thornton (6)
Buck and Spitz did this (5)
Buck had to _____ with many owners; leave (4)
Buck killed this leader-dog (5)
Buck's California owner (6)
Buck's ignorant owner from the south (7)
Buck's last master-friend (8)
Buck, for example (3)
Camp from which one goes out (4)
Charles's wife (8)
Charles, Hal & Mercedes are killed trying to cross one (5)
Chilly; opposite of hot (4)
Color of blood and sweater (3)
Dog at John's camp (3)
Dog's feet (4)
Dogs have to work hard when it is deep (4)
Dogs worked together (4)
Frozen water (3)
Gardener's helper; sold Buck (6)
Go - Command (4)
Go right or left (4)
He worked with Francois (8)
Hearing organ (3)
Indian tribe (7)

It holds dogs together and to the sled (7)
Job of the Scott half-breed: ___ Train (4)
Large animal Buck killed (5)
Man in the red _____ (7)
Mercedes' brother (3)
Mr. Miller's official title (5)
Name means angry one (7)
Not part of everyone (3)
One who steals (5)
Opposite of North (5)
Opposite of live (3)
Past tense of eat (3)
Ripped (4)
Spitz killed this Newfoundland (5)
Stop - Command (2)
The Law Buck learned: Club and ___ (4)
The man in the read sweater had one (4)
Thing the dogs pulled (4)
Thornton's friend (6)
To take _____ in one's work (5)
Traits of dogs; _____ to their owners (7)
What Indians called Buck: ___ Dog (5)
Where John and Buck went (5)
Wolves _____ at the moon (4)
Worked with Perrault (8)
Yellow metal discovered in the North (4)
You _____ the whip to keep order (3)
_____ of the fittest (8)

The Call of the Wild Word Search 1 Answer Key

Animal(s) Buck met in Wilderness (4)
Black Burton _____ John Thornton (3)
Black _____; Buck killed him for hitting Thornton (6)
Buck and Spitz did this (5)
Buck had to _____ with many owners; leave (4)
Buck killed this leader-dog (5)
Buck's California owner (6)
Buck's ignorant owner from the south (7)
Buck's last master-friend (8)
Buck, for example (3)
Camp from which one goes out (4)
Charles's wife (8)
Charles, Hal & Mercedes are killed trying to cross one (5)
Chilly; opposite of hot (4)
Color of blood and sweater (3)
Dog at John's camp (3)
Dog's feet (4)
Dogs have to work hard when it is deep (4)
Dogs worked together (4)
Frozen water (3)
Gardener's helper; sold Buck (6)
Go - Command (4)
Go right or left (4)
He worked with Francois (8)
Hearing organ (3)
Indian tribe (7)

It holds dogs together and to the sled (7)
Job of the Scott half-breed: ___ Train (4)
Large animal Buck killed (5)
Man in the red _____ (7)
Mercedes' brother (3)
Mr. Miller's official title (5)
Name means angry one (7)
Not part of everyone (3)
One who steals (5)
Opposite of North (5)
Opposite of live (3)
Past tense of eat (3)
Ripped (4)
Spitz killed this Newfoundland (5)
Stop - Command (2)
The Law Buck learned: Club and ___ (4)
The man in the read sweater had one (4)
Thing the dogs pulled (4)
Thornton's friend (6)
To take _____ in one's work (5)
Traits of dogs; _____ to their owners (7)
What Indians called Buck: ___ Dog (5)
Where John and Buck went (5)
Wolves _____ at the moon (4)
Worked with Perrault (8)
Yellow metal discovered in the North (4)
You _____ the whip to keep order (3)
_____ of the fittest (8)

The Call of the Wild Word Search 2

```
H O H I T S O H G F L Z H N J W H R T
S M Q C K C L N L Y I T N A X O T I H
U L R E L M H O S N Y G E P L O U V O
M A Y C I F W A Q S F T H A U D O E R
E S W E A T E R R W Y H G T M S S R N
S L F N M L S V D L G K O N B I E N T
O E G P S B L L R N E G L W O L D I O
O D C L U B O U D O G S D C L L I G N
M T P R R C C Q P N W T N I E P R Z T
H F T T V Y H T H T F A M U C A P G H
L O D O I J U D G E R N N E I R B O G
N O D R V W X V I F V A H G F T S R G
H E Y N A T H H W J M G J D X T C Y Y
R A N A L C T T T N D T A N A U B R S
P B R T L U A R R E P I T H R R S K V
X A A N Z T M E R C E D E S B N H P H
M F W S E J Y F H T L E T Q O T D R Q
K Q W S E S B B X N Y S M W F X Q D R
S P I T Z J S O L L E K S Q V X T Y N
```

Animal(s) Buck met in Wilderness (4)
Black Burton _____ John Thornton (3)
Black _____; Buck killed him for hitting Thornton (6)
Buck and Spitz did this (5)
Buck had to _____ with many owners; leave (4)
Buck killed this leader-dog (5)
Buck's California owner (6)
Buck's ignorant owner from the south (7)
Buck's last master-friend (8)
Buck, for example (3)
Camp from which one goes out (4)
Charles's wife (8)
Charles, Hal & Mercedes are killed trying to cross one (5)
Chilly; opposite of hot (4)
Color of blood and sweater (3)
Dog at John's camp (3)
Dog's feet (4)
Dogs have to work hard when it is deep (4)
Dogs worked together (4)
Frozen water (3)
Gardener's helper; sold Buck (6)
Go - Command (4)
Go right or left (4)
He worked with Francois (8)
Hearing organ (3)
Indian tribe (7)

It holds dogs together and to the sled (7)
Job of the Scott half-breed: ___ Train (4)
Large animal Buck killed (5)
Man in the red _____ (7)
Mercedes' brother (3)
Mr. Miller's official title (5)
Name means angry one (7)
Not part of everyone (3)
One who steals (5)
Opposite of North (5)
Opposite of live (3)
Past tense of eat (3)
Ripped (4)
Spitz killed this Newfoundland (5)
Stop - Command (2)
The Law Buck learned: Club and ___ (4)
The man in the read sweater had one (4)
Thing the dogs pulled (4)
Thornton's friend (6)
To take _____ in one's work (5)
Traits of dogs; _____ to their owners (7)
What Indians called Buck: ___ Dog (5)
Where John and Buck went (5)
Wolves _____ at the moon (4)
Worked with Perrault (8)
Yellow metal discovered in the North (4)
You _____ the whip to keep order (3)
_____ of the fittest (8)

The Call of the Wild Word Search 2 Answer Key

```
H O H I T S O H G F       H       W H R T
S   C   C       L   I T   E   A   O T I H
U   R E L   H O     G     H   L U D O V O
M A   I F W A       A U T M   S   O E R
E S W E A T E R R Y H G   O     I   S N T
S L   N M L   D L     L W O L D   I   O
O E G S B L L R E   S D C L   P R G N
O D C L U B O U D O G S   N I E P
M   R R C C       F A M U   A
    T T V   J U D G E R N E I R B O
L O   O I         I F   A       T S
N O D R V       H       M       A
H E Y N A       T       D A   A U
R A   A L               A T H   R S
P B R T L U A R R E P I T H E S N
    A A N   T M E R C E D E S
    W S E   Y           E       O
      S E S             Y   W
S P I T Z       S O L L E K S
```

Animal(s) Buck met in Wilderness (4)
Black Burton _____ John Thornton (3)
Black _____; Buck killed him for hitting Thornton (6)
Buck and Spitz did this (5)
Buck had to _____ with many owners; leave (4)
Buck killed this leader-dog (5)
Buck's California owner (6)
Buck's ignorant owner from the south (7)
Buck's last master-friend (8)
Buck, for example (3)
Camp from which one goes out (4)
Charles's wife (8)
Charles, Hal & Mercedes are killed trying to cross one (5)
Chilly; opposite of hot (4)
Color of blood and sweater (3)
Dog at John's camp (3)
Dog's feet (4)
Dogs have to work hard when it is deep (4)
Dogs worked together (4)
Frozen water (3)
Gardener's helper; sold Buck (6)
Go - Command (4)
Go right or left (4)
He worked with Francois (8)
Hearing organ (3)
Indian tribe (7)

It holds dogs together and to the sled (7)
Job of the Scott half-breed: ___ Train (4)
Large animal Buck killed (5)
Man in the red _____ (7)
Mercedes' brother (3)
Mr. Miller's official title (5)
Name means angry one (7)
Not part of everyone (3)
One who steals (5)
Opposite of North (5)
Opposite of live (3)
Past tense of eat (3)
Ripped (4)
Spitz killed this Newfoundland (5)
Stop - Command (2)
The Law Buck learned: Club and ___ (4)
The man in the read sweater had one (4)
Thing the dogs pulled (4)
Thornton's friend (6)
To take _____ in one's work (5)
Traits of dogs; _____ to their owners (7)
What Indians called Buck: ___ Dog (5)
Where John and Buck went (5)
Wolves _____ at the moon (4)
Worked with Perrault (8)
Yellow metal discovered in the North (4)
You _____ the whip to keep order (3)
_____ of the fittest (8)

The Call of the Wild Word Search 3

```
F H H A W O O D S N E M Z L S O U T H B
L A C T X H B S T G M B A K S R Y S F P
O G N E T R M P D X Z C E I P I K O R N
W D X G H Y M U K D H L N P L V Z H A N
G J J D O O J X J A L D X Y A E Y G N W
Z S X D R F W K R O C G G Q V R F X C F
W W V R N J Z L S B T D H J I K R M O B
Y L P T D E B U R T O N R V L K C I N
T V T D O S G B Z Z Z N H T R Y P X S G
L N M X N G D V P S D M J W U D V M K W
H D S Z T H W J C W Y G W D S N E P T P
Y Q W B C A R P W Z E M R B D R E F Y C
M W E R T R D F W Y E A K R C R M C H T
Q P A C C N K Z D S H N C E R Q S U P D
F A T L F E R E Y N A U D A M J P R R N
H R E U I S L M B O T E U E H M I L I L
O T R B G S N P A W S L O Y A L T Y D W
D M U O H R I S Y U T C T E L R Z L E T
A K D R T K G F K Z Z Z T H D I O S Y R
D L O G N E I R B O B A S E I C M U H H
X X L V R R C J L F J V R L E E G B H V
T O R N M I L L E R M O O S E W F H I T
```

ALL	FANG	JUDGE	PAWS	SWEATER
ATE	FIGHT	LOYALTY	PERRAULT	TEAM
BASE	FRANCOIS	MAIL	PRIDE	THIEF
BURTON	GHOST	MANUEL	RED	THORNTON
CHARLES	GOLD	MERCEDES	RIVER	TORN
CLUB	HAL	MILLER	SLED	TURN
COLD	HARNESS	MOOSE	SNOW	USE
CURLY	HIT	MUSH	SOLLEKS	WOLF
DIE	HO	NIG	SOUTH	WOODS
DOG	HOWL	OBRIEN	SPITZ	YEEHATS
EAR	ICE	PART	SURVIVAL	

The Call of the Wild Word Search 3 Answer Key

ALL	FANG	JUDGE	PAWS	SWEATER
ATE	FIGHT	LOYALTY	PERRAULT	TEAM
BASE	FRANCOIS	MAIL	PRIDE	THIEF
BURTON	GHOST	MANUEL	RED	THORNTON
CHARLES	GOLD	MERCEDES	RIVER	TORN
CLUB	HAL	MILLER	SLED	TURN
COLD	HARNESS	MOOSE	SNOW	USE
CURLY	HIT	MUSH	SOLLEKS	WOLF
DIE	HO	NIG	SOUTH	WOODS
DOG	HOWL	OBRIEN	SPITZ	YEEHATS
EAR	ICE	PART	SURVIVAL	

The Call of the Wild Word Search 4

```
S U R V I V A L S W T H H D O G H D E R
G R J M S Q R Q O W S O V J T D L T B S
F J I U F J G N Y U E F R B Y O A D L V
F B K V D J S C M K Z A N N G R V V B M
B A Z M E G Q Q N G J T T W O O D S D G
T J N R W R E N C X G T D E W F T R M D
V W W G M L P W D T J M N H R Y Z X V V
R M S V J E T W Y R M J H M M S M G Q R
S I O C N A R F P E R A U L T M A I L
R R F P T Y S C S T N P R D Q Z Y Q T H
P Y G F R S T T E V N M N T V C T D X M
Z N M Q R I Q H L D T O E S F L P E D T
T M P T H R D I A I E O S O L U A C R S
G C U R L Y E E H A T S S H O B R I E N
D C G C K J I F V U L E O G W X T L D N
S F T H B D T J R E U R A L M J R K O M
Y O T J G K H N D F M S B M L A J T J R
T B U R T O N S P I T Z E L H E N I G Q
M X D T W Q R R L G E T L C X R K U M W
M L B L H Z Q L C H A A W P O V Z S E G L
B A S E P G E V H T R S H H P A W S C L
C O L D B R Y L O Y A L T Y V W N Q S Y
```

ALL	FANG	JUDGE	PAWS	SWEATER
ATE	FIGHT	LOYALTY	PERRAULT	TEAM
BASE	FRANCOIS	MAIL	PRIDE	THIEF
BURTON	GHOST	MANUEL	RED	THORNTON
CHARLES	GOLD	MERCEDES	RIVER	TORN
CLUB	HAL	MILLER	SLED	TURN
COLD	HARNESS	MOOSE	SNOW	USE
CURLY	HIT	MUSH	SOLLEKS	WOLF
DIE	HO	NIG	SOUTH	WOODS
DOG	HOWL	OBRIEN	SPITZ	YEEHATS
EAR	ICE	PART	SURVIVAL	

The Call of the Wild Word Search 4 Answer Key

ALL	FANG	JUDGE	PAWS	SWEATER
ATE	FIGHT	LOYALTY	PERRAULT	TEAM
BASE	FRANCOIS	MAIL	PRIDE	THIEF
BURTON	GHOST	MANUEL	RED	THORNTON
CHARLES	GOLD	MERCEDES	RIVER	TORN
CLUB	HAL	MILLER	SLED	TURN
COLD	HARNESS	MOOSE	SNOW	USE
CURLY	HIT	MUSH	SOLLEKS	WOLF
DIE	HO	NIG	SOUTH	WOODS
DOG	HOWL	OBRIEN	SPITZ	YEEHATS
EAR	ICE	PART	SURVIVAL	

The Call of the Wild Crossword 1

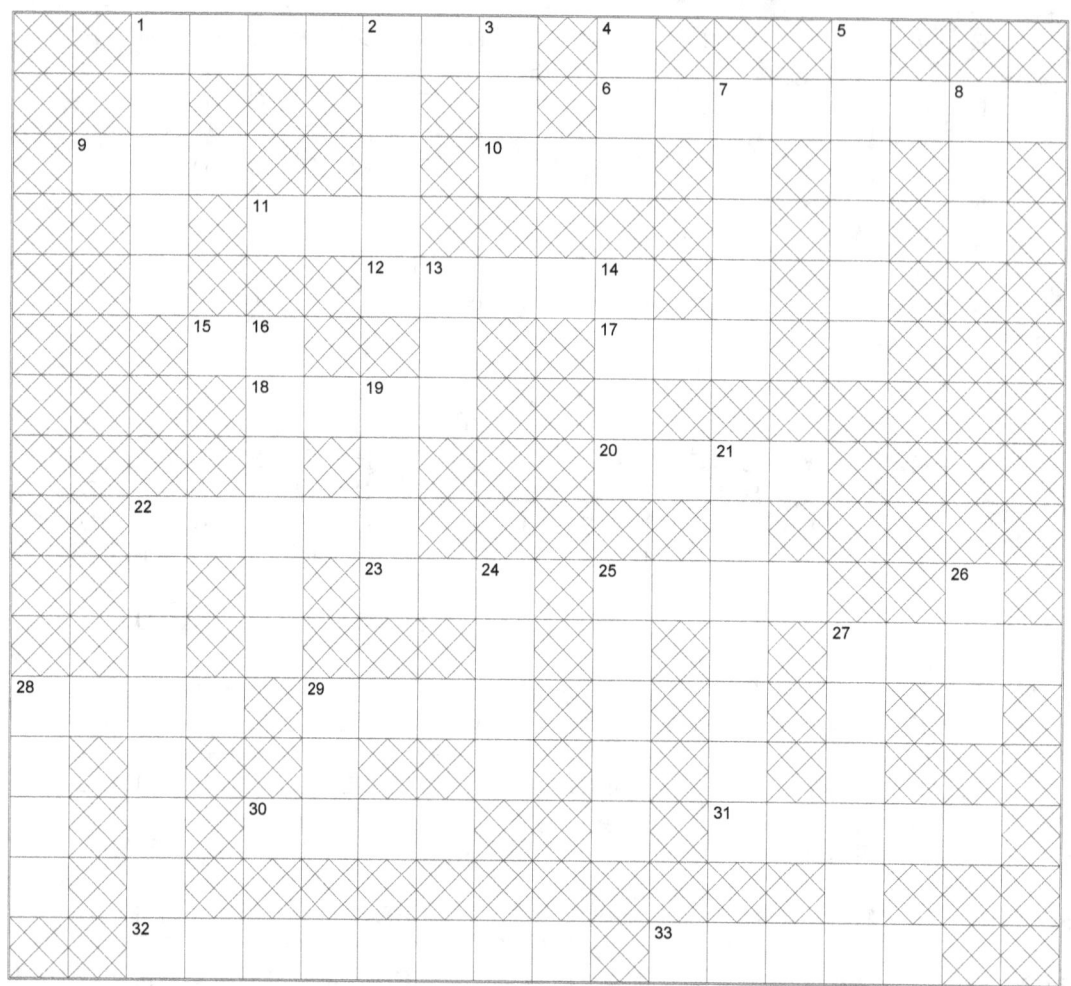

Across
1. Man in the red _____
6. _____ of the fittest
9. Black Burton _____ John Thornton
10. Opposite of live
11. Past tense of eat
12. Buck and Spitz did this
15. Stop - Command
17. Hearing organ
18. Camp from which one goes out
20. Go - Command
22. To take _____ in one's work
23. Buck, for example
25. Animal(s) Buck met in Wilderness
27. Job of the Scott half-breed: ___ Train
28. Go right or left
29. Wolves _____ at the moon
30. The man in the read sweater had one
31. Opposite of North
32. Buck's last master-friend
33. Spitz killed this Newfoundland

Down
1. Buck killed this leader-dog
2. One who steals
3. Color of blood and sweater
4. You _____ the whip to keep order
5. Buck's California owner
7. Charles, Hal & Mercedes are killed trying to cross one
8. Not part of everyone
13. Frozen water
14. Dogs worked together
16. Thornton's friend
19. Thing the dogs pulled
21. Name means angry one
22. He worked with Francois
24. Yellow metal discovered in the North
25. Where John and Buck went
26. Dog at John's camp
27. Gardener's helper; sold Buck
28. Ripped
29. Mercedes' brother

The Call of the Wild Crossword 1 Answer Key

		1 S	W	E	A	2 T	E	3 R		4 U			5 M		
		P				H		E		6 S	U	7 R	V	I	V	A	8 L
	9 H	I	T			I		10 D	I	E		I		L		L
	I			11 A	T	E						V		L		L
	T			Z		12 F	13 I	G	H	14 T		E		E		
			15 H	16 O			C			17 E	A	R		R		
				18 B	A	19 S	E			A						
				R		L				20 M	U	21 S	H			
		22 P	R	I	D	E						O				
		E				23 D	24 O	25 G		W	O	L	F		26 N	
		R		E			N			O		L		27 M	A	I	L
28 T	U	R	N		29 H	O	W	L		O		E		A		G
O		A			A			D		D		K		N		
R		U		30 C	L	U	B			S		31 S	O	U	T	H
N		L										E				
		32 T	H	O	R	N	T	O	N		33 C	U	R	L	Y	

Across
1. Man in the red _____
6. _____ of the fittest
9. Black Burton _____ John Thornton
10. Opposite of live
11. Past tense of eat
12. Buck and Spitz did this
15. Stop - Command
17. Hearing organ
18. Camp from which one goes out
20. Go - Command
22. To take _____ in one's work
23. Buck, for example
25. Animal(s) Buck met in Wilderness
27. Job of the Scott half-breed: ___ Train
28. Go right or left
29. Wolves _____ at the moon
30. The man in the read sweater had one
31. Opposite of North
32. Buck's last master-friend
33. Spitz killed this Newfoundland

Down
1. Buck killed this leader-dog
2. One who steals
3. Color of blood and sweater
4. You _____ the whip to keep order
5. Buck's California owner
7. Charles, Hal & Mercedes are killed trying to cross one
8. Not part of everyone
13. Frozen water
14. Dogs worked together
16. Thornton's friend
19. Thing the dogs pulled
21. Name means angry one
22. He worked with Francois
24. Yellow metal discovered in the North
25. Where John and Buck went
26. Dog at John's camp
27. Gardener's helper; sold Buck
28. Ripped
29. Mercedes' brother

The Call of the Wild Crossword 2

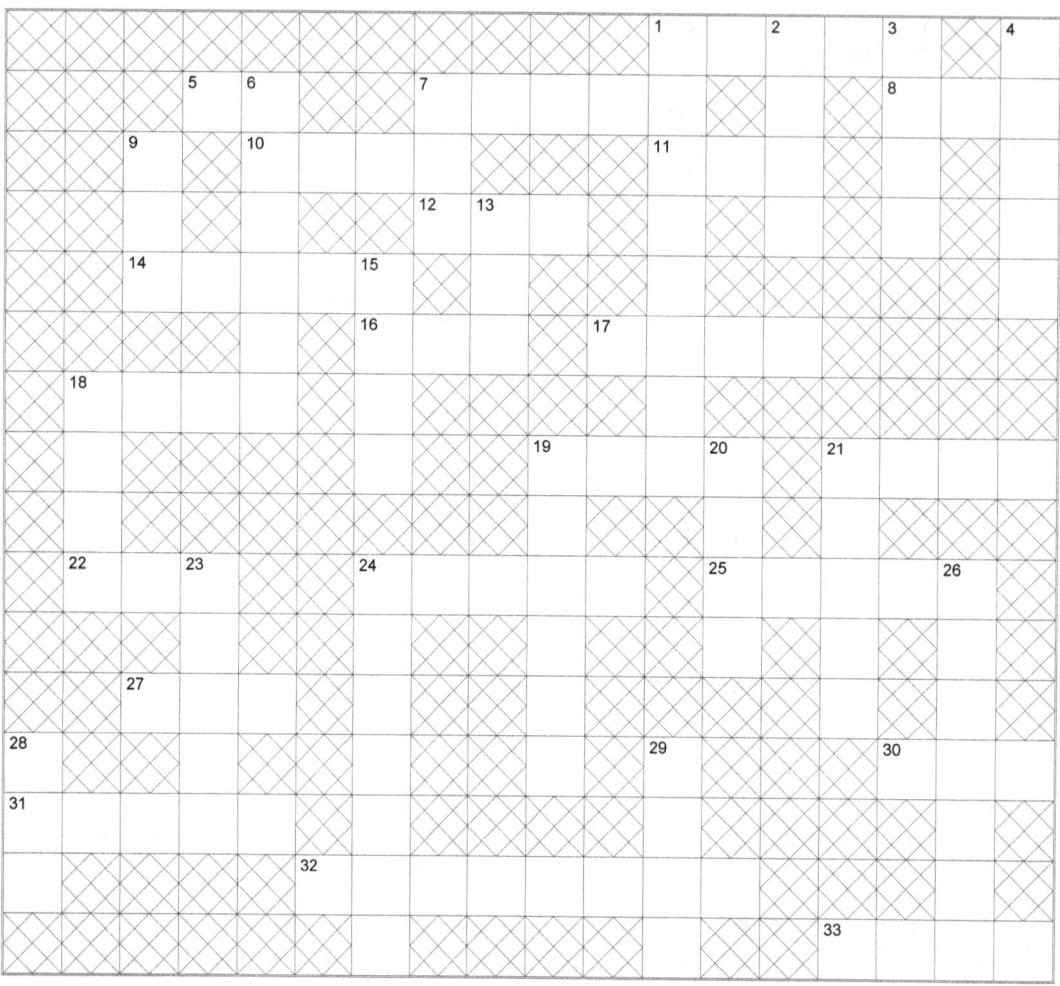

Across
1. Buck and Spitz did this
5. Stop - Command
7. Charles, Hal & Mercedes are killed trying to cross one
8. Hearing organ
10. Camp from which one goes out
11. Not part of everyone
12. Opposite of live
14. One who steals
16. Past tense of eat
17. Animal(s) Buck met in Wilderness
18. Go right or left
19. Go - Command
21. Job of the Scott half-breed: ___ Train
22. Dog at John's camp
24. Spitz killed this Newfoundland
25. Where John and Buck went
27. Buck, for example
30. Mercedes' brother
31. Buck killed this leader-dog
32. Charles's wife
33. Buck had to _____ with many owners; leave

Down
1. Worked with Perrault
2. Yellow metal discovered in the North
3. Dogs worked together
4. To take _____ in one's work
6. Thornton's friend
7. Color of blood and sweater
9. Black Burton _____ John Thornton
13. Frozen water
15. The Law Buck learned: Club and ___
18. Ripped
19. Buck's California owner
20. Wolves _____ at the moon
21. Large animal Buck killed
23. What Indians called Buck: ___ Dog
24. Buck's ignorant owner from the south
26. Man in the red _____
28. You _____ the whip to keep order
29. Thing the dogs pulled

The Call of the Wild Crossword 2 Answer Key

								¹F	²I	³G	H	T		⁴P
		⁵H	⁶O		⁷R	I	V	E	R		O		⁸E	A	R
	⁹H		¹⁰B	A	S	E		¹¹A	L	L			A		I
	I		R			¹²D	¹³I	E		N			M		D
	¹⁴T	H	I	E	¹⁵F		C			C					E
			E		¹⁶A	T	E		¹⁷W	O	L	F			
	¹⁸T	U	R	N		N			I						
	O				G			¹⁹M	U	S	²⁰H		²¹M	A	I	L
	R							I			O		O		
	²²N	I	²³G		²⁴C	U	R	L	Y		²⁵W	O	O	D	²⁶S
			H		H			L			L		S		W
		²⁷D	O	G		A		E					E		E
²⁸U		S			R			²⁹S			³⁰H	A	L
³¹S	P	I	T	Z		L			L				T	
E					³²M	E	R	C	E	D	E	S		E
						S				D			³³P	A	R	T

Across
1. Buck and Spitz did this
5. Stop - Command
7. Charles, Hal & Mercedes are killed trying to cross one
8. Hearing organ
10. Camp from which one goes out
11. Not part of everyone
12. Opposite of live
14. One who steals
16. Past tense of eat
17. Animal(s) Buck met in Wilderness
18. Go right or left
19. Go - Command
21. Job of the Scott half-breed: ___ Train
22. Dog at John's camp
24. Spitz killed this Newfoundland
25. Where John and Buck went
27. Buck, for example
30. Mercedes' brother
31. Buck killed this leader-dog
32. Charles's wife
33. Buck had to _____ with many owners; leave

Down
1. Worked with Perrault
2. Yellow metal discovered in the North
3. Dogs worked together
4. To take _____ in one's work
6. Thornton's friend
7. Color of blood and sweater
9. Black Burton _____ John Thornton
13. Frozen water
15. The Law Buck learned: Club and ___
18. Ripped
19. Buck's California owner
20. Wolves _____ at the moon
21. Large animal Buck killed
23. What Indians called Buck: ___ Dog
24. Buck's ignorant owner from the south
26. Man in the red _____
28. You _____ the whip to keep order
29. Thing the dogs pulled

The Call of the Wild Crossword 3

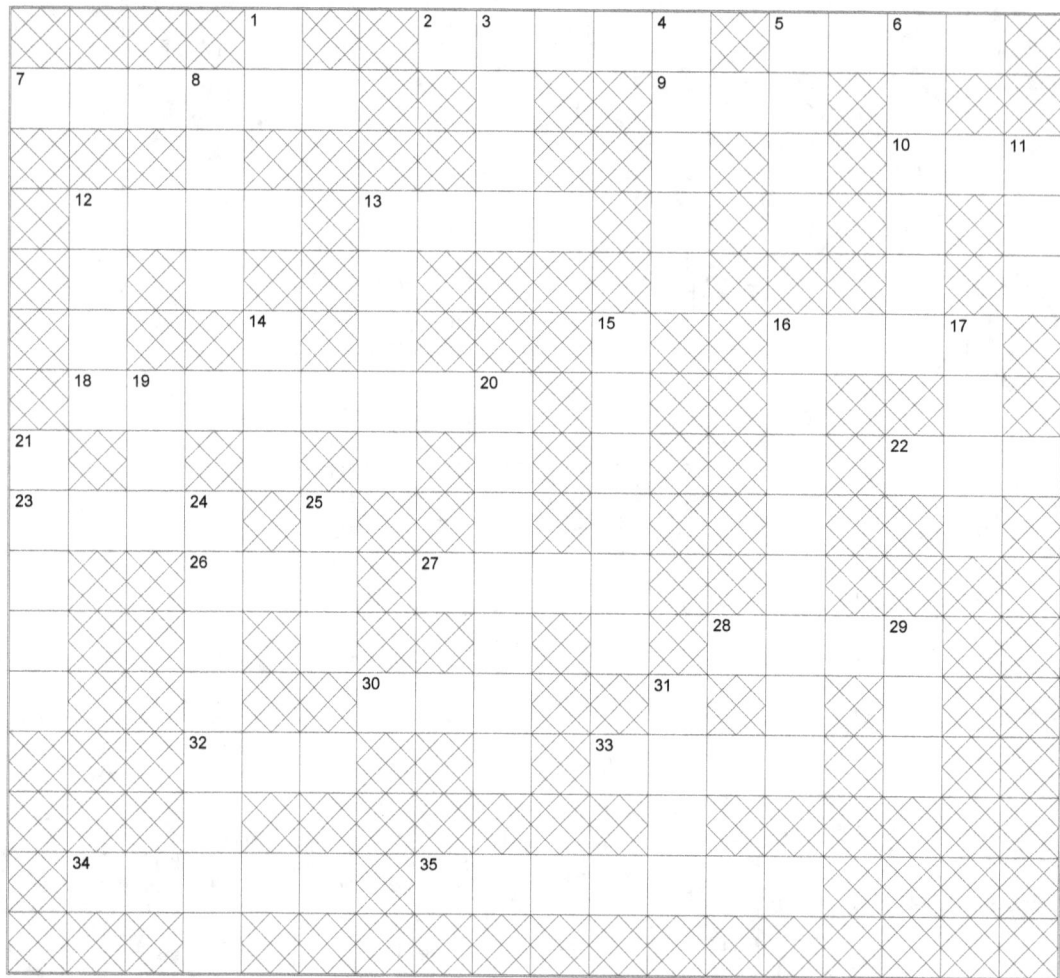

Across
2. What Indians called Buck: ___ Dog
5. Dogs have to work hard when it is deep
7. Black _____; Buck killed him for hitting Thornton
9. Mercedes' brother
10. Color of blood and sweater
12. Go right or left
13. Animal(s) Buck met in Wilderness
16. The Law Buck learned: Club and ___
18. Charles's wife
22. Not part of everyone
23. Buck had to _____ with many owners; leave
26. Black Burton _____ John Thornton
27. Camp from which one goes out
28. Chilly; opposite of hot
30. You _____ the whip to keep order
32. Dog at John's camp
33. Dog's feet
34. Large animal Buck killed
35. Buck's ignorant owner from the south

Down
1. Stop - Command
3. Wolves _____ at the moon
4. One who steals
5. Thing the dogs pulled
6. Thornton's friend
8. Ripped
11. Opposite of live
12. Dogs worked together
13. Where John and Buck went
14. Frozen water
15. Buck's California owner
16. Worked with Perrault
17. Yellow metal discovered in the North
19. Hearing organ
20. Man in the red _____
21. Buck killed this leader-dog
24. Buck's last master-friend
25. Past tense of eat
29. Buck, for example
31. Job of the Scott half-breed: ___ Train

The Call of the Wild Crossword 3 Answer Key

			1 H		2 G	3 H	4 S		5 S	N	6 O	W	
7 B	U	R	T	O	N		O		9 H	A	L	B	
			O			W		I		E		10 R	11 D
	12 T	U	R	N		13 W	O	L	F	E	D	I	I
	E		N			O		F			16	E	E
	A			14 I		O		15 M		F	A	17 N	G
	18 M	19 E	R	C	E	D	20 E	S	I		R		O
21 S		A		E		S	W		L		A	22 A	L	L
23 P	A	R	24 T		25 A		E		L		N		D
I			26 H	I	T		27 B	A	S	E		C	
T			O		E		T		R		28 C	O	L	29 D
Z			R			30 U	S	E		31 M		I		O
			32 N	I	G			R		33 P	A	W	S	G
			T							I				
			34 M	O	O	S	E	35 C	H	A	R	L	E	S
			N											

Across
- 2. What Indians called Buck: ___ Dog
- 5. Dogs have to work hard when it is deep
- 7. Black _____; Buck killed him for hitting Thornton
- 9. Mercedes' brother
- 10. Color of blood and sweater
- 12. Go right or left
- 13. Animal(s) Buck met in Wilderness
- 16. The Law Buck learned: Club and ___
- 18. Charles's wife
- 22. Not part of everyone
- 23. Buck had to _____ with many owners; leave
- 26. Black Burton _____ John Thornton
- 27. Camp from which one goes out
- 28. Chilly; opposite of hot
- 30. You _____ the whip to keep order
- 32. Dog at John's camp
- 33. Dog's feet
- 34. Large animal Buck killed
- 35. Buck's ignorant owner from the south

Down
- 1. Stop - Command
- 3. Wolves _____ at the moon
- 4. One who steals
- 5. Thing the dogs pulled
- 6. Thornton's friend
- 8. Ripped
- 11. Opposite of live
- 12. Dogs worked together
- 13. Where John and Buck went
- 14. Frozen water
- 15. Buck's California owner
- 16. Worked with Perrault
- 17. Yellow metal discovered in the North
- 19. Hearing organ
- 20. Man in the red _____
- 21. Buck killed this leader-dog
- 24. Buck's last master-friend
- 25. Past tense of eat
- 29. Buck, for example
- 31. Job of the Scott half-breed: ___ Train

The Call of the Wild Crossword 4

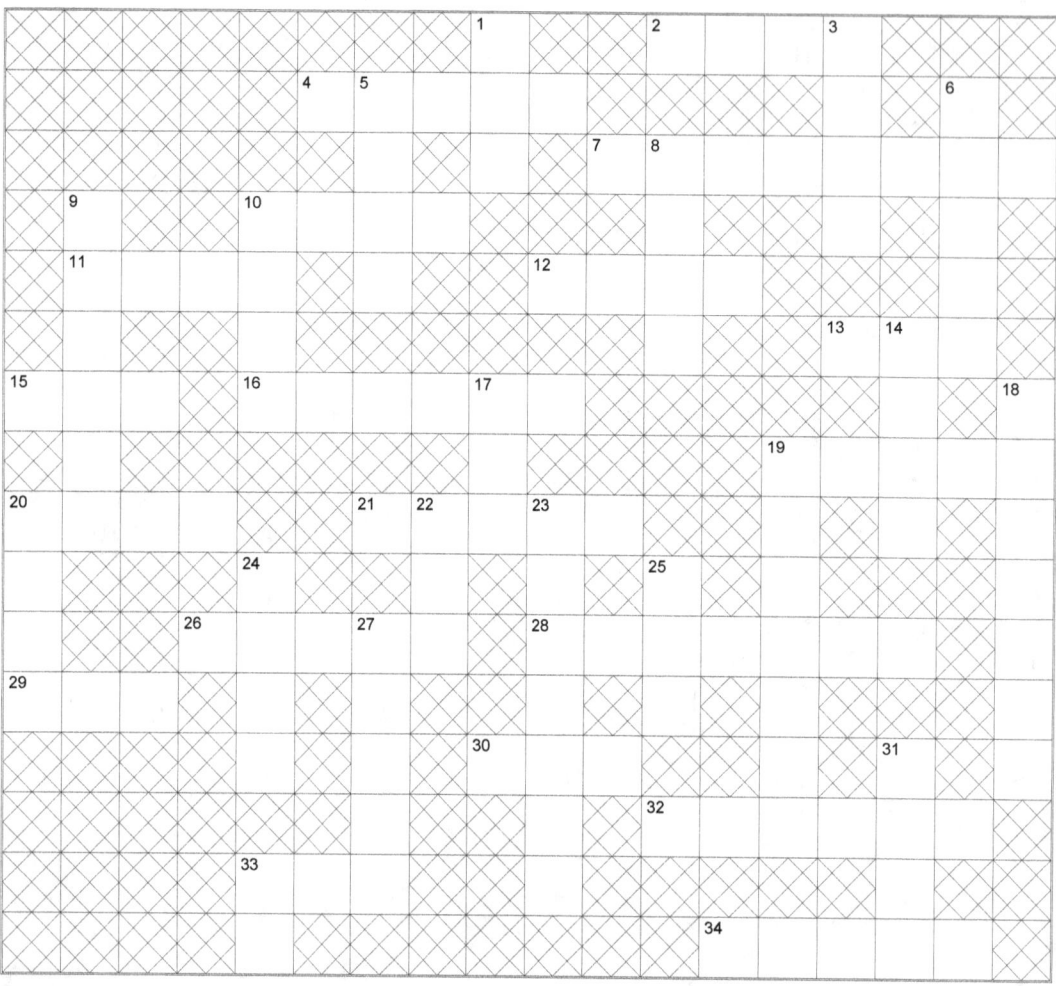

Across
2. Animal(s) Buck met in Wilderness
4. Buck killed this leader-dog
7. Buck's last master-friend
10. Ripped
11. Camp from which one goes out
12. Dog's feet
13. Frozen water
15. Dog at John's camp
16. Buck's California owner
19. Opposite of North
20. Dogs have to work hard when it is deep
21. Spitz killed this Newfoundland
26. Mr. Miller's official title
28. Indian tribe
29. Opposite of live
30. Not part of everyone
32. Black _____; Buck killed him for hitting Thornton
33. Black Burton _____ John Thornton
34. Where John and Buck went

Down
1. Past tense of eat
3. The Law Buck learned: Club and ___
5. Buck had to _____ with many owners; leave
6. Large animal Buck killed
8. Wolves _____ at the moon
9. Thornton's friend
10. Dogs worked together
14. The man in the read sweater had one
17. Hearing organ
18. Buck's ignorant owner from the south
19. Man in the red _____
20. Thing the dogs pulled
22. You _____ the whip to keep order
23. Traits of dogs; _____ to their owners
24. Go right or left
25. Color of blood and sweater
27. What Indians called Buck: ___ Dog
31. Chilly; opposite of hot
33. Stop - Command

The Call of the Wild Crossword 4 Answer Key

							¹A		²W	O	L	³F		
				⁴S	⁵P	I	T	Z				A		⁶M
					A		E		⁷T	⁸H	O	R	N	T	O	N
	⁹O		¹⁰T	O	R	N				O			G		O
	¹¹B	A	S	E		T		¹²P	A	W	S			¹³I	¹⁴C	E
		R				A				L				
¹⁵N	I	G		¹⁶M	I	L	L	¹⁷E	R				L		¹⁸C
	E							A			¹⁹S	O	U	T	H
²⁰S	N	O	W		²¹C	²²U	R	²³L	Y		W		B		A
L				²⁴T		S		O		²⁵R	E				R
E		²⁶J	U	D	²⁷G	E		²⁸Y	E	E	H	A	T	S	L
²⁹D	I	E		R	H			A		D		T		³¹C	E
				N	O		³⁰A	L	L		E			C	S
					S			T		³²B	U	R	T	O	N
				³³H	I	T		Y					L	
				O					³⁴W	O	O	D	S	

Across
2. Animal(s) Buck met in Wilderness
4. Buck killed this leader-dog
7. Buck's last master-friend
10. Ripped
11. Camp from which one goes out
12. Dog's feet
13. Frozen water
15. Dog at John's camp
16. Buck's California owner
19. Opposite of North
20. Dogs have to work hard when it is deep
21. Spitz killed this Newfoundland
26. Mr. Miller's official title
28. Indian tribe
29. Opposite of live
30. Not part of everyone
32. Black _____; Buck killed him for hitting Thornton
33. Black Burton _____ John Thornton
34. Where John and Buck went

Down
1. Past tense of eat
3. The Law Buck learned: Club and ___
5. Buck had to _____ with many owners; leave
6. Large animal Buck killed
8. Wolves _____ at the moon
9. Thornton's friend
10. Dogs worked together
14. The man in the read sweater had one
17. Hearing organ
18. Buck's ignorant owner from the south
19. Man in the red _____
20. Thing the dogs pulled
22. You _____ the whip to keep order
23. Traits of dogs; _____ to their owners
24. Go right or left
25. Color of blood and sweater
27. What Indians called Buck: ___ Dog
31. Chilly; opposite of hot
33. Stop - Command

The Call of the Wild

COLD	DOG	NIG	SOUTH	YEEHATS
BASE	RED	SPITZ	ICE	JUDGE
TORN	ATE	FREE SPACE	DIE	SNOW
CHARLES	MUSH	THORNTON	BURTON	SWEATER
MILLER	CLUB	TURN	MOOSE	FIGHT

The Call of the Wild

SOLLEKS	FRANCOIS	TEAM	CURLY	MANUEL
HARNESS	HIT	HAL	PART	THIEF
ALL	MERCEDES	FREE SPACE	HO	EAR
GHOST	RIVER	MAIL	USE	HOWL
LOYALTY	WOLF	PRIDE	OBRIEN	PERRAULT

The Call of the Wild

HARNESS	SLED	FIGHT	LOYALTY	COLD
BASE	TORN	HO	THIEF	SURVIVAL
ICE	NIG	FREE SPACE	SWEATER	CLUB
MERCEDES	GHOST	OBRIEN	CHARLES	BURTON
PERRAULT	ALL	TEAM	ATE	PRIDE

The Call of the Wild

MUSH	MANUEL	DIE	MILLER	JUDGE
WOODS	GOLD	SPITZ	PAWS	MAIL
SNOW	YEEHATS	FREE SPACE	FRANCOIS	RED
RIVER	FANG	EAR	USE	HOWL
DOG	CURLY	TURN	THORNTON	MOOSE

The Call of the Wild

BURTON	SPITZ	YEEHATS	SURVIVAL	SWEATER
MAIL	GHOST	COLD	HARNESS	PRIDE
DIE	PAWS	FREE SPACE	FRANCOIS	SLED
PERRAULT	MERCEDES	ICE	LOYALTY	NIG
MANUEL	WOLF	MOOSE	DOG	THORNTON

The Call of the Wild

HOWL	BASE	RED	PART	MUSH
CURLY	FANG	ALL	TURN	FIGHT
TORN	GOLD	FREE SPACE	HO	MILLER
WOODS	ATE	SOLLEKS	CHARLES	SNOW
OBRIEN	RIVER	JUDGE	TEAM	USE

The Call of the Wild

WOLF	THORNTON	JUDGE	USE	GOLD
ICE	SOLLEKS	HOWL	ALL	MILLER
BASE	SWEATER	FREE SPACE	THIEF	SNOW
TORN	TURN	SOUTH	ATE	HO
WOODS	PAWS	RIVER	HAL	MAIL

The Call of the Wild

OBRIEN	DOG	SPITZ	PART	YEEHATS
CURLY	HIT	MUSH	NIG	EAR
CLUB	MANUEL	FREE SPACE	SLED	SURVIVAL
PRIDE	CHARLES	HARNESS	GHOST	PERRAULT
RED	TEAM	DIE	FIGHT	MERCEDES

The Call of the Wild

HOWL	PERRAULT	TORN	HAL	THORNTON
ATE	SNOW	WOODS	PART	SWEATER
HO	ICE	FREE SPACE	SOLLEKS	DOG
USE	FANG	CHARLES	YEEHATS	COLD
JUDGE	THIEF	FIGHT	SURVIVAL	OBRIEN

The Call of the Wild

PAWS	LOYALTY	SPITZ	MILLER	FRANCOIS
CLUB	MERCEDES	MOOSE	CURLY	GHOST
RIVER	MUSH	FREE SPACE	MANUEL	NIG
BASE	ALL	BURTON	SLED	TURN
DIE	RED	PRIDE	EAR	MAIL

The Call of the Wild

DOG	SNOW	HO	MUSH	SOUTH
EAR	CURLY	NIG	FANG	MILLER
BASE	DIE	FREE SPACE	MANUEL	TORN
SURVIVAL	GHOST	RED	RIVER	USE
HIT	ALL	FIGHT	MAIL	TEAM

The Call of the Wild

SOLLEKS	CHARLES	THIEF	PART	SWEATER
MERCEDES	YEEHATS	BURTON	COLD	GOLD
HAL	HARNESS	FREE SPACE	PAWS	TURN
MOOSE	JUDGE	ICE	THORNTON	PRIDE
PERRAULT	HOWL	LOYALTY	OBRIEN	SPITZ

The Call of the Wild

TURN	MUSH	USE	JUDGE	HO
CURLY	LOYALTY	PERRAULT	THIEF	ALL
HAL	WOODS	FREE SPACE	CLUB	ATE
MERCEDES	SWEATER	HARNESS	SLED	PRIDE
HIT	DIE	RIVER	SPITZ	ICE

The Call of the Wild

RED	TEAM	NIG	MAIL	SOUTH
CHARLES	DOG	PART	BASE	THORNTON
BURTON	WOLF	FREE SPACE	FIGHT	MILLER
HOWL	COLD	TORN	MOOSE	SOLLEKS
SURVIVAL	FRANCOIS	OBRIEN	FANG	YEEHATS

The Call of the Wild

CHARLES	USE	JUDGE	WOLF	SOUTH
HARNESS	MILLER	TEAM	HO	SURVIVAL
NIG	EAR	FREE SPACE	TORN	PRIDE
MOOSE	COLD	PERRAULT	OBRIEN	HOWL
ICE	MAIL	BURTON	WOODS	DOG

The Call of the Wild

SWEATER	MUSH	SPITZ	GOLD	CURLY
MANUEL	THORNTON	SNOW	HIT	FANG
RED	SOLLEKS	FREE SPACE	CLUB	HAL
FIGHT	DIE	ATE	TURN	YEEHATS
ALL	FRANCOIS	THIEF	PART	SLED

The Call of the Wild

CHARLES	ICE	MILLER	MANUEL	WOODS
SURVIVAL	HOWL	RED	MOOSE	HARNESS
COLD	WOLF	FREE SPACE	SWEATER	GHOST
JUDGE	HO	ALL	SNOW	HIT
EAR	PRIDE	GOLD	FIGHT	SLED

The Call of the Wild

TURN	LOYALTY	BURTON	CURLY	OBRIEN
YEEHATS	ATE	SPITZ	PAWS	MERCEDES
USE	NIG	FREE SPACE	DIE	TORN
SOUTH	THIEF	RIVER	MAIL	THORNTON
CLUB	SOLLEKS	MUSH	PART	TEAM

The Call of the Wild

PERRAULT	DOG	MUSH	JUDGE	MANUEL
MAIL	CLUB	WOLF	SOLLEKS	SOUTH
THIEF	NIG	FREE SPACE	USE	FRANCOIS
GOLD	YEEHATS	DIE	RED	PRIDE
SWEATER	ALL	RIVER	CURLY	BURTON

The Call of the Wild

PART	SNOW	BASE	COLD	EAR
MOOSE	GHOST	OBRIEN	ATE	MERCEDES
HAL	PAWS	FREE SPACE	WOODS	SLED
CHARLES	THORNTON	FIGHT	SPITZ	TORN
HARNESS	HO	HIT	FANG	ICE

The Call of the Wild

HOWL	THORNTON	DOG	MOOSE	SNOW
SOUTH	TORN	PRIDE	SLED	HARNESS
SWEATER	WOODS	FREE SPACE	HIT	ALL
COLD	ATE	OBRIEN	MUSH	NIG
FIGHT	BURTON	SOLLEKS	SURVIVAL	YEEHATS

The Call of the Wild

CLUB	MERCEDES	PERRAULT	JUDGE	LOYALTY
PART	TEAM	ICE	SPITZ	CHARLES
THIEF	FRANCOIS	FREE SPACE	DIE	CURLY
FANG	HAL	GHOST	RED	MILLER
MANUEL	USE	BASE	TURN	RIVER

The Call of the Wild

MUSH	GHOST	SOLLEKS	HAL	FRANCOIS
BASE	COLD	PERRAULT	SWEATER	RED
FIGHT	BURTON	FREE SPACE	MERCEDES	MOOSE
THIEF	MANUEL	PRIDE	HARNESS	NIG
EAR	DIE	MAIL	SPITZ	ALL

The Call of the Wild

GOLD	ICE	ATE	TEAM	CHARLES
PART	JUDGE	LOYALTY	OBRIEN	CLUB
SOUTH	HIT	FREE SPACE	YEEHATS	SLED
TORN	WOLF	SNOW	MILLER	FANG
USE	WOODS	RIVER	HOWL	TURN

The Call of the Wild

PART	MOOSE	COLD	USE	SOLLEKS
CURLY	HARNESS	THIEF	NIG	SLED
ICE	MERCEDES	FREE SPACE	FRANCOIS	PAWS
LOYALTY	HIT	HAL	SWEATER	CLUB
RED	JUDGE	SPITZ	WOLF	HO

The Call of the Wild

CHARLES	BURTON	TORN	RIVER	DIE
MANUEL	YEEHATS	ALL	EAR	WOODS
MAIL	DOG	FREE SPACE	ATE	GOLD
FANG	THORNTON	TURN	OBRIEN	HOWL
SNOW	FIGHT	TEAM	PRIDE	SOUTH

The Call of the Wild

RIVER	USE	SOUTH	ALL	RED
WOLF	HOWL	FRANCOIS	FIGHT	ICE
GHOST	COLD	FREE SPACE	PAWS	PRIDE
HIT	HO	TEAM	HAL	THORNTON
MUSH	HARNESS	EAR	SNOW	DOG

The Call of the Wild

BURTON	MAIL	OBRIEN	GOLD	THIEF
LOYALTY	TORN	JUDGE	SLED	PART
TURN	MANUEL	FREE SPACE	CHARLES	SPITZ
BASE	NIG	CURLY	DIE	CLUB
SOLLEKS	SURVIVAL	MILLER	PERRAULT	ATE

The Call of the Wild

FRANCOIS	SPITZ	PAWS	FIGHT	FANG
RED	MUSH	GOLD	THORNTON	CHARLES
ALL	CURLY	FREE SPACE	SNOW	PERRAULT
ATE	LOYALTY	HIT	HOWL	WOLF
EAR	BURTON	SOLLEKS	SLED	DIE

The Call of the Wild

GHOST	SWEATER	MERCEDES	SURVIVAL	YEEHATS
OBRIEN	PRIDE	THIEF	DOG	RIVER
MILLER	PART	FREE SPACE	JUDGE	BASE
HAL	MANUEL	USE	NIG	MAIL
HO	CLUB	TURN	TORN	TEAM

The Call of the Wild

HAL	MANUEL	ICE	CHARLES	HIT
MOOSE	TEAM	RED	MERCEDES	PRIDE
SOUTH	MAIL	FREE SPACE	PAWS	YEEHATS
MUSH	PART	ALL	DOG	FANG
HO	HARNESS	USE	TURN	CLUB

The Call of the Wild

GHOST	GOLD	JUDGE	MILLER	SWEATER
SLED	FIGHT	PERRAULT	WOODS	LOYALTY
BASE	EAR	FREE SPACE	TORN	HOWL
DIE	RIVER	FRANCOIS	ATE	NIG
SNOW	SURVIVAL	THORNTON	COLD	THIEF

The Call of the Wild Vocabulary Word List

No.	Word	Clue/Definition
1.	APPEASE	to pacify, to tranquilize
2.	APPREHENSIVELY	fearfully, suspiciously
3.	ARDUOUS	difficult, laborious
4.	ASPIRED	to aim at high things
5.	ASSAILED	attacked, assaulted
6.	CALLOWNESS	immature, unsophisticated
7.	CERTITUDE	infallible, unmistakable
8.	CONSPICUOUS	clearly in view, distinguishable
9.	COPIOUS	abundant
10.	COVERT	secret, private
11.	DAUNTED	discouraged, intimidated
12.	DEFIED	challenged, provoked to combat
13.	DEFT	apt, clever
14.	EXPLOIT	heroic act, deed of renown
15.	FORMIDABLE	difficult to deal with
16.	FUTILELY	serving no useful purpose
17.	IMPEDE	to hamper, obstruct
18.	IMPERIOUSLY	domineering, arrogant
19.	IMPLORINGLY	beseech, pray for earnestly
20.	IMPORTUNED	to urge repeatedly
21.	INCARNATE	give a concrete or actual form to
22.	INDISPENSABLE	necessary, essential
23.	LATENT	under the surface, hidden
24.	PALPITANT	trembling or throbbing
25.	PRIMORDIAL	original, earliest formed
26.	PROVOCATION	something that stimulates anger
27.	REALM	a region
28.	REMNANT	a scrap, fragment, remaining
29.	REPUGNANCE	aversion, dislike, reluctance
30.	RETALIATED	to take revenge, reprisal
31.	REVELATION	astonishing disclosure
32.	SWARTHY	dark complexion
33.	TANGIBLE	something that can be touched, actual
34.	TRANSIENT	fleeting, momentary
35.	VORACIOUS	ravenous

Copyrighted

The Call of the Wild Vocabulary Fill In The Blanks 1

_____ 1. heroic act, deed of renown

_____ 2. something that can be touched, actual

_____ 3. give a concrete or actual form to

_____ 4. beseech, pray for earnestly

_____ 5. secret, private

_____ 6. a region

_____ 7. difficult to deal with

_____ 8. fleeting, momentary

_____ 9. discouraged, intimidated

_____ 10. dark complexion

_____ 11. under the surface, hidden

_____ 12. to take revenge, reprisal

_____ 13. to pacify, to tranquilize

_____ 14. difficult, laborious

_____ 15. attacked, assaulted

_____ 16. a scrap, fragment, remaining

_____ 17. aversion, dislike, reluctance

_____ 18. to hamper, obstruct

_____ 19. necessary, essential

_____ 20. abundant

The Call of the Wild Vocabulary Fill In The Blanks 1 Answer Key

EXPLOIT	1. heroic act, deed of renown
TANGIBLE	2. something that can be touched, actual
INCARNATE	3. give a concrete or actual form to
IMPLORINGLY	4. beseech, pray for earnestly
COVERT	5. secret, private
REALM	6. a region
FORMIDABLE	7. difficult to deal with
TRANSIENT	8. fleeting, momentary
DAUNTED	9. discouraged, intimidated
SWARTHY	10. dark complexion
LATENT	11. under the surface, hidden
RETALIATED	12. to take revenge, reprisal
APPEASE	13. to pacify, to tranquilize
ARDUOUS	14. difficult, laborious
ASSAILED	15. attacked, assaulted
REMNANT	16. a scrap, fragment, remaining
REPUGNANCE	17. aversion, dislike, reluctance
IMPEDE	18. to hamper, obstruct
INDISPENSABLE	19. necessary, essential
COPIOUS	20. abundant

The Call of the Wild Vocabulary Fill In The Blanks 2

_____

_____

_____

_____

_____

_____

_____

_____

_____

_____

_____

_____

_____

_____

_____

_____

_____

_____

_____

_____

1. beseech, pray for earnestly
2. astonishing disclosure
3. necessary, essential
4. to urge repeatedly
5. trembling or throbbing
6. original, earliest formed
7. something that stimulates anger
8. apt, clever
9. to aim at high things
10. heroic act, deed of renown
11. abundant
12. a scrap, fragment, remaining
13. to pacify, to tranquilize
14. under the surface, hidden
15. attacked, assaulted
16. secret, private
17. serving no useful purpose
18. infallible, unmistakable
19. to hamper, obstruct
20. fleeting, momentary

The Call of the Wild Vocabulary Fill In The Blanks 2 Answer Key

IMPLORINGLY	1. beseech, pray for earnestly
REVELATION	2. astonishing disclosure
INDISPENSABLE	3. necessary, essential
IMPORTUNED	4. to urge repeatedly
PALPITANT	5. trembling or throbbing
PRIMORDIAL	6. original, earliest formed
PROVOCATION	7. something that stimulates anger
DEFT	8. apt, clever
ASPIRED	9. to aim at high things
EXPLOIT	10. heroic act, deed of renown
COPIOUS	11. abundant
REMNANT	12. a scrap, fragment, remaining
APPEASE	13. to pacify, to tranquilize
LATENT	14. under the surface, hidden
ASSAILED	15. attacked, assaulted
COVERT	16. secret, private
FUTILELY	17. serving no useful purpose
CERTITUDE	18. infallible, unmistakable
IMPEDE	19. to hamper, obstruct
TRANSIENT	20. fleeting, momentary

The Call of the Wild Vocabulary Fill In The Blanks 3

_____ 1. dark complexion

_____ 2. something that can be touched, actual

_____ 3. secret, private

_____ 4. original, earliest formed

_____ 5. to take revenge, reprisal

_____ 6. a region

_____ 7. fearfully, suspiciously

_____ 8. beseech, pray for earnestly

_____ 9. to urge repeatedly

_____ 10. abundant

_____ 11. trembling or throbbing

_____ 12. discouraged, intimidated

_____ 13. a scrap, fragment, remaining

_____ 14. clearly in view, distinguishable

_____ 15. under the surface, hidden

_____ 16. domineering, arrogant

_____ 17. apt, clever

_____ 18. challenged, provoked to combat

_____ 19. necessary, essential

_____ 20. to aim at high things

The Call of the Wild Vocabulary Fill In The Blanks 3 Answer Key

SWARTHY	1. dark complexion
TANGIBLE	2. something that can be touched, actual
COVERT	3. secret, private
PRIMORDIAL	4. original, earliest formed
RETALIATED	5. to take revenge, reprisal
REALM	6. a region
APPREHENSIVELY	7. fearfully, suspiciously
IMPLORINGLY	8. beseech, pray for earnestly
IMPORTUNED	9. to urge repeatedly
COPIOUS	10. abundant
PALPITANT	11. trembling or throbbing
DAUNTED	12. discouraged, intimidated
REMNANT	13. a scrap, fragment, remaining
CONSPICUOUS	14. clearly in view, distinguishable
LATENT	15. under the surface, hidden
IMPERIOUSLY	16. domineering, arrogant
DEFT	17. apt, clever
DEFIED	18. challenged, provoked to combat
INDISPENSABLE	19. necessary, essential
ASPIRED	20. to aim at high things

The Call of the Wild Vocabulary Fill In The Blanks 4

1. difficult to deal with
2. to aim at high things
3. heroic act, deed of renown
4. something that stimulates anger
5. difficult, laborious
6. serving no useful purpose
7. discouraged, intimidated
8. something that can be touched, actual
9. dark complexion
10. a scrap, fragment, remaining
11. to take revenge, reprisal
12. challenged, provoked to combat
13. beseech, pray for earnestly
14. fearfully, suspiciously
15. under the surface, hidden
16. to hamper, obstruct
17. abundant
18. infallible, unmistakable
19. a region
20. to pacify, to tranquilize

The Call of the Wild Vocabulary Fill In The Blanks 4 Answer Key

FORMIDABLE	1. difficult to deal with
ASPIRED	2. to aim at high things
EXPLOIT	3. heroic act, deed of renown
PROVOCATION	4. something that stimulates anger
ARDUOUS	5. difficult, laborious
FUTILELY	6. serving no useful purpose
DAUNTED	7. discouraged, intimidated
TANGIBLE	8. something that can be touched, actual
SWARTHY	9. dark complexion
REMNANT	10. a scrap, fragment, remaining
RETALIATED	11. to take revenge, reprisal
DEFIED	12. challenged, provoked to combat
IMPLORINGLY	13. beseech, pray for earnestly
APPREHENSIVELY	14. fearfully, suspiciously
LATENT	15. under the surface, hidden
IMPEDE	16. to hamper, obstruct
COPIOUS	17. abundant
CERTITUDE	18. infallible, unmistakable
REALM	19. a region
APPEASE	20. to pacify, to tranquilize

The Call of the Wild Vocabulary Matching 1

___ 1. APPEASE   A. to hamper, obstruct
___ 2. CERTITUDE   B. infallible, unmistakable
___ 3. DEFT   C. under the surface, hidden
___ 4. FORMIDABLE   D. to pacify, to tranquilize
___ 5. PRIMORDIAL   E. difficult, laborious
___ 6. PALPITANT   F. a region
___ 7. COPIOUS   G. discouraged, intimidated
___ 8. IMPEDE   H. trembling or throbbing
___ 9. FUTILELY   I. apt, clever
___10. LATENT   J. to urge repeatedly
___11. IMPERIOUSLY   K. give a concrete or actual form to
___12. SWARTHY   L. to aim at high things
___13. APPREHENSIVELY M. original, earliest formed
___14. INDISPENSABLE   N. necessary, essential
___15. INCARNATE   O. dark complexion
___16. COVERT   P. serving no useful purpose
___17. IMPORTUNED   Q. secret, private
___18. RETALIATED   R. abundant
___19. REALM   S. difficult to deal with
___20. REVELATION   T. heroic act, deed of renown
___21. TRANSIENT   U. to take revenge, reprisal
___22. ASPIRED   V. astonishing disclosure
___23. ARDUOUS   W. fearfully, suspiciously
___24. DAUNTED   X. domineering, arrogant
___25. EXPLOIT   Y. fleeting, momentary

The Call of the Wild Vocabulary Matching 1 Answer Key

D - 1. APPEASE   A. to hamper, obstruct
B - 2. CERTITUDE   B. infallible, unmistakable
I - 3. DEFT   C. under the surface, hidden
S - 4. FORMIDABLE   D. to pacify, to tranquilize
M - 5. PRIMORDIAL   E. difficult, laborious
H - 6. PALPITANT   F. a region
R - 7. COPIOUS   G. discouraged, intimidated
A - 8. IMPEDE   H. trembling or throbbing
P - 9. FUTILELY   I. apt, clever
C - 10. LATENT   J. to urge repeatedly
X - 11. IMPERIOUSLY   K. give a concrete or actual form to
O - 12. SWARTHY   L. to aim at high things
W - 13. APPREHENSIVELY   M. original, earliest formed
N - 14. INDISPENSABLE   N. necessary, essential
K - 15. INCARNATE   O. dark complexion
Q - 16. COVERT   P. serving no useful purpose
J - 17. IMPORTUNED   Q. secret, private
U - 18. RETALIATED   R. abundant
F - 19. REALM   S. difficult to deal with
V - 20. REVELATION   T. heroic act, deed of renown
Y - 21. TRANSIENT   U. to take revenge, reprisal
L - 22. ASPIRED   V. astonishing disclosure
E - 23. ARDUOUS   W. fearfully, suspiciously
G - 24. DAUNTED   X. domineering, arrogant
T - 25. EXPLOIT   Y. fleeting, momentary

The Call of the Wild Vocabulary Matching 2

___ 1. LATENT
___ 2. VORACIOUS
___ 3. INCARNATE
___ 4. IMPORTUNED
___ 5. REMNANT
___ 6. ASSAILED
___ 7. ARDUOUS
___ 8. IMPEDE
___ 9. APPREHENSIVELY
___ 10. PRIMORDIAL
___ 11. RETALIATED
___ 12. APPEASE
___ 13. ASPIRED
___ 14. EXPLOIT
___ 15. REALM
___ 16. IMPLORINGLY
___ 17. INDISPENSABLE
___ 18. DEFT
___ 19. REPUGNANCE
___ 20. TRANSIENT
___ 21. FUTILELY
___ 22. SWARTHY
___ 23. DAUNTED
___ 24. IMPERIOUSLY
___ 25. PALPITANT

A. apt, clever
B. fearfully, suspiciously
C. to hamper, obstruct
D. heroic act, deed of renown
E. to pacify, to tranquilize
F. a scrap, fragment, remaining
G. original, earliest formed
H. a region
I. serving no useful purpose
J. give a concrete or actual form to
K. attacked, assaulted
L. difficult, laborious
M. fleeting, momentary
N. to take revenge, reprisal
O. trembling or throbbing
P. to aim at high things
Q. beseech, pray for earnestly
R. ravenous
S. dark complexion
T. discouraged, intimidated
U. to urge repeatedly
V. aversion, dislike, reluctance
W. domineering, arrogant
X. under the surface, hidden
Y. necessary, essential

The Call of the Wild Vocabulary Matching 2 Answer Key

X - 1. LATENT		A. apt, clever
R - 2. VORACIOUS		B. fearfully, suspiciously
J - 3. INCARNATE		C. to hamper, obstruct
U - 4. IMPORTUNED		D. heroic act, deed of renown
F - 5. REMNANT		E. to pacify, to tranquilize
K - 6. ASSAILED		F. a scrap, fragment, remaining
L - 7. ARDUOUS		G. original, earliest formed
C - 8. IMPEDE		H. a region
B - 9. APPREHENSIVELY		I. serving no useful purpose
G - 10. PRIMORDIAL		J. give a concrete or actual form to
N - 11. RETALIATED		K. attacked, assaulted
E - 12. APPEASE		L. difficult, laborious
P - 13. ASPIRED		M. fleeting, momentary
D - 14. EXPLOIT		N. to take revenge, reprisal
H - 15. REALM		O. trembling or throbbing
Q - 16. IMPLORINGLY		P. to aim at high things
Y - 17. INDISPENSABLE		Q. beseech, pray for earnestly
A - 18. DEFT		R. ravenous
V - 19. REPUGNANCE		S. dark complexion
M - 20. TRANSIENT		T. discouraged, intimidated
I - 21. FUTILELY		U. to urge repeatedly
S - 22. SWARTHY		V. aversion, dislike, reluctance
T - 23. DAUNTED		W. domineering, arrogant
W - 24. IMPERIOUSLY		X. under the surface, hidden
O - 25. PALPITANT		Y. necessary, essential

The Call of the Wild Vocabulary Matching 3

___ 1. PRIMORDIAL   A. discouraged, intimidated
___ 2. TANGIBLE   B. abundant
___ 3. COPIOUS   C. to aim at high things
___ 4. DAUNTED   D. heroic act, deed of renown
___ 5. CALLOWNESS   E. fearfully, suspiciously
___ 6. EXPLOIT   F. something that can be touched, actual
___ 7. IMPORTUNED   G. dark complexion
___ 8. REALM   H. to take revenge, reprisal
___ 9. TRANSIENT   I. to hamper, obstruct
___10. CONSPICUOUS   J. original, earliest formed
___11. IMPERIOUSLY   K. aversion, dislike, reluctance
___12. SWARTHY   L. apt, clever
___13. IMPEDE   M. something that stimulates anger
___14. FORMIDABLE   N. challenged, provoked to combat
___15. ASSAILED   O. domineering, arrogant
___16. LATENT   P. beseech, pray for earnestly
___17. DEFIED   Q. to urge repeatedly
___18. DEFT   R. under the surface, hidden
___19. REPUGNANCE   S. fleeting, momentary
___20. IMPLORINGLY   T. a region
___21. APPREHENSIVELY   U. clearly in view, distinguishable
___22. VORACIOUS   V. difficult to deal with
___23. ASPIRED   W. attacked, assaulted
___24. PROVOCATION   X. immature, unsophisticated
___25. RETALIATED   Y. ravenous

The Call of the Wild Vocabulary Matching 3 Answer Key

J - 1. PRIMORDIAL
F - 2. TANGIBLE
B - 3. COPIOUS
A - 4. DAUNTED
X - 5. CALLOWNESS
D - 6. EXPLOIT
Q - 7. IMPORTUNED
T - 8. REALM
S - 9. TRANSIENT
U - 10. CONSPICUOUS
O - 11. IMPERIOUSLY
G - 12. SWARTHY
I - 13. IMPEDE
V - 14. FORMIDABLE
W - 15. ASSAILED
R - 16. LATENT
N - 17. DEFIED
L - 18. DEFT
K - 19. REPUGNANCE
P - 20. IMPLORINGLY
E - 21. APPREHENSIVELY
Y - 22. VORACIOUS
C - 23. ASPIRED
M - 24. PROVOCATION
H - 25. RETALIATED

A. discouraged, intimidated
B. abundant
C. to aim at high things
D. heroic act, deed of renown
E. fearfully, suspiciously
F. something that can be touched, actual
G. dark complexion
H. to take revenge, reprisal
I. to hamper, obstruct
J. original, earliest formed
K. aversion, dislike, reluctance
L. apt, clever
M. something that stimulates anger
N. challenged, provoked to combat
O. domineering, arrogant
P. beseech, pray for earnestly
Q. to urge repeatedly
R. under the surface, hidden
S. fleeting, momentary
T. a region
U. clearly in view, distinguishable
V. difficult to deal with
W. attacked, assaulted
X. immature, unsophisticated
Y. ravenous

The Call of the Wild Vocabulary Matching 4

___ 1. DEFIED   A. something that can be touched, actual
___ 2. ASSAILED   B. discouraged, intimidated
___ 3. APPREHENSIVELY C. something that stimulates anger
___ 4. VORACIOUS   D. apt, clever
___ 5. RETALIATED   E. ravenous
___ 6. COVERT   F. challenged, provoked to combat
___ 7. PRIMORDIAL   G. clearly in view, distinguishable
___ 8. CERTITUDE   H. original, earliest formed
___ 9. TANGIBLE   I. give a concrete or actual form to
___ 10. DEFT   J. infallible, unmistakable
___ 11. DAUNTED   K. to pacify, to tranquilize
___ 12. INDISPENSABLE L. fleeting, momentary
___ 13. REVELATION   M. domineering, arrogant
___ 14. COPIOUS   N. to take revenge, reprisal
___ 15. LATENT   O. difficult, laborious
___ 16. ARDUOUS   P. astonishing disclosure
___ 17. REMNANT   Q. abundant
___ 18. IMPERIOUSLY   R. necessary, essential
___ 19. PROVOCATION   S. fearfully, suspiciously
___ 20. PALPITANT   T. under the surface, hidden
___ 21. INCARNATE   U. trembling or throbbing
___ 22. APPEASE   V. a region
___ 23. TRANSIENT   W. attacked, assaulted
___ 24. CONSPICUOUS   X. secret, private
___ 25. REALM   Y. a scrap, fragment, remaining

The Call of the Wild Vocabulary Matching 4 Answer Key

F - 1. DEFIED	A.	something that can be touched, actual
W - 2. ASSAILED	B.	discouraged, intimidated
S - 3. APPREHENSIVELY	C.	something that stimulates anger
E - 4. VORACIOUS	D.	apt, clever
N - 5. RETALIATED	E.	ravenous
X - 6. COVERT	F.	challenged, provoked to combat
H - 7. PRIMORDIAL	G.	clearly in view, distinguishable
J - 8. CERTITUDE	H.	original, earliest formed
A - 9. TANGIBLE	I.	give a concrete or actual form to
D - 10. DEFT	J.	infallible, unmistakable
B - 11. DAUNTED	K.	to pacify, to tranquilize
R - 12. INDISPENSABLE	L.	fleeting, momentary
P - 13. REVELATION	M.	domineering, arrogant
Q - 14. COPIOUS	N.	to take revenge, reprisal
T - 15. LATENT	O.	difficult, laborious
O - 16. ARDUOUS	P.	astonishing disclosure
Y - 17. REMNANT	Q.	abundant
M - 18. IMPERIOUSLY	R.	necessary, essential
C - 19. PROVOCATION	S.	fearfully, suspiciously
U - 20. PALPITANT	T.	under the surface, hidden
I - 21. INCARNATE	U.	trembling or throbbing
K - 22. APPEASE	V.	a region
L - 23. TRANSIENT	W.	attacked, assaulted
G - 24. CONSPICUOUS	X.	secret, private
V - 25. REALM	Y.	a scrap, fragment, remaining

The Call of the Wild Vocabulary Magic Squares 1

Match the definition with the vocabulary word. Put your answers in the magic squares below. When your answers are correct, all columns and rows will add to the same number.

A. APPREHENSIVELY
B. PALPITANT
C. DEFIED
D. IMPERIOUSLY
E. INDISPENSABLE
F. INCARNATE
G. PRIMORDIAL
H. ASSAILED
I. REALM
J. LATENT
K. IMPEDE
L. COVERT
M. TRANSIENT
N. COPIOUS
O. ASPIRED
P. APPEASE

1. trembling or throbbing
2. original, earliest formed
3. to hamper, obstruct
4. abundant
5. fleeting, momentary
6. secret, private
7. attacked, assaulted
8. fearfully, suspiciously
9. to pacify, to tranquilize
10. a region
11. necessary, essential
12. domineering, arrogant
13. challenged, provoked to combat
14. give a concrete or actual form to
15. under the surface, hidden
16. to aim at high things

A=	B=	C=	D=
E=	F=	G=	H=
I=	J=	K=	L=
M=	N=	O=	P=

The Call of the Wild Vocabulary Magic Squares 1 Answer Key

Match the definition with the vocabulary word. Put your answers in the magic squares below. When your answers are correct, all columns and rows will add to the same number.

A. APPREHENSIVELY
B. PALPITANT
C. DEFIED
D. IMPERIOUSLY
E. INDISPENSABLE
F. INCARNATE
G. PRIMORDIAL
H. ASSAILED
I. REALM
J. LATENT
K. IMPEDE
L. COVERT
M. TRANSIENT
N. COPIOUS
O. ASPIRED
P. APPEASE

1. trembling or throbbing
2. original, earliest formed
3. to hamper, obstruct
4. abundant
5. fleeting, momentary
6. secret, private
7. attacked, assaulted
8. fearfully, suspiciously
9. to pacify, to tranquilize
10. a region
11. necessary, essential
12. domineering, arrogant
13. challenged, provoked to combat
14. give a concrete or actual form to
15. under the surface, hidden
16. to aim at high things

A=8	B=1	C=13	D=12
E=11	F=14	G=2	H=7
I=10	J=15	K=3	L=6
M=5	N=4	O=16	P=9

The Call of the Wild Vocabulary Magic Squares 2

Match the definition with the vocabulary word. Put your answers in the magic squares below. When your answers are correct, all columns and rows will add to the same number.

A. TRANSIENT
B. DEFT
C. RETALIATED
D. REMNANT
E. SWARTHY
F. COVERT
G. CONSPICUOUS
H. IMPERIOUSLY
I. APPEASE
J. ASPIRED
K. REPUGNANCE
L. COPIOUS
M. DEFIED
N. CALLOWNESS
O. PRIMORDIAL
P. IMPORTUNED

1. fleeting, momentary
2. immature, unsophisticated
3. to aim at high things
4. dark complexion
5. clearly in view, distinguishable
6. abundant
7. to urge repeatedly
8. to take revenge, reprisal
9. original, earliest formed
10. a scrap, fragment, remaining
11. domineering, arrogant
12. aversion, dislike, reluctance
13. to pacify, to tranquilize
14. secret, private
15. apt, clever
16. challenged, provoked to combat

A=	B=	C=	D=
E=	F=	G=	H=
I=	J=	K=	L=
M=	N=	O=	P=

The Call of the Wild Vocabulary Magic Squares 2 Answer Key

Match the definition with the vocabulary word. Put your answers in the magic squares below. When your answers are correct, all columns and rows will add to the same number.

A. TRANSIENT
B. DEFT
C. RETALIATED
D. REMNANT
E. SWARTHY
F. COVERT
G. CONSPICUOUS
H. IMPERIOUSLY
I. APPEASE
J. ASPIRED
K. REPUGNANCE
L. COPIOUS
M. DEFIED
N. CALLOWNESS
O. PRIMORDIAL
P. IMPORTUNED

1. fleeting, momentary
2. immature, unsophisticated
3. to aim at high things
4. dark complexion
5. clearly in view, distinguishable
6. abundant
7. to urge repeatedly
8. to take revenge, reprisal
9. original, earliest formed
10. a scrap, fragment, remaining
11. domineering, arrogant
12. aversion, dislike, reluctance
13. to pacify, to tranquilize
14. secret, private
15. apt, clever
16. challenged, provoked to combat

A=1	B=15	C=8	D=10
E=4	F=14	G=5	H=11
I=13	J=3	K=12	L=6
M=16	N=2	O=9	P=7

The Call of the Wild Vocabulary Magic Squares 3

Match the definition with the vocabulary word. Put your answers in the magic squares below. When your answers are correct, all columns and rows will add to the same number.

A. RETALIATED
B. DEFT
C. ASSAILED
D. REALM
E. REPUGNANCE
F. LATENT
G. DAUNTED
H. FORMIDABLE
I. ASPIRED
J. PRIMORDIAL
K. APPREHENSIVELY
L. ARDUOUS
M. CONSPICUOUS
N. PROVOCATION
O. EXPLOIT
P. SWARTHY

1. clearly in view, distinguishable
2. under the surface, hidden
3. difficult to deal with
4. heroic act, deed of renown
5. difficult, laborious
6. attacked, assaulted
7. to take revenge, reprisal
8. original, earliest formed
9. fearfully, suspiciously
10. a region
11. apt, clever
12. to aim at high things
13. something that stimulates anger
14. aversion, dislike, reluctance
15. discouraged, intimidated
16. dark complexion

A= 7	B= 11	C= 6	D= 10
E= 14	F= 2	G= 15	H= 3
I= 12	J= 8	K= 9	L= 5
M= 1	N= 13	O= 4	P= 16

The Call of the Wild Vocabulary Magic Squares 3 Answer Key

Match the definition with the vocabulary word. Put your answers in the magic squares below. When your answers are correct, all columns and rows will add to the same number.

A. RETALIATED
B. DEFT
C. ASSAILED
D. REALM
E. REPUGNANCE
F. LATENT
G. DAUNTED
H. FORMIDABLE
I. ASPIRED
J. PRIMORDIAL
K. APPREHENSIVELY
L. ARDUOUS
M. CONSPICUOUS
N. PROVOCATION
O. EXPLOIT
P. SWARTHY

1. clearly in view, distinguishable
2. under the surface, hidden
3. difficult to deal with
4. heroic act, deed of renown
5. difficult, laborious
6. attacked, assaulted
7. to take revenge, reprisal
8. original, earliest formed
9. fearfully, suspiciously
10. a region
11. apt, clever
12. to aim at high things
13. something that stimulates anger
14. aversion, dislike, reluctance
15. discouraged, intimidated
16. dark complexion

A=7	B=11	C=6	D=10
E=14	F=2	G=15	H=3
I=12	J=8	K=9	L=5
M=1	N=13	O=4	P=16

The Call of the Wild Vocabulary Magic Squares 4

Match the definition with the vocabulary word. Put your answers in the magic squares below. When your answers are correct, all columns and rows will add to the same number.

A. IMPERIOUSLY
B. CALLOWNESS
C. EXPLOIT
D. TANGIBLE
E. INCARNATE
F. PRIMORDIAL
G. APPREHENSIVELY
H. SWARTHY
I. REPUGNANCE
J. LATENT
K. DEFIED
L. CONSPICUOUS
M. FORMIDABLE
N. IMPLORINGLY
O. IMPORTUNED
P. APPEASE

1. to urge repeatedly
2. something that can be touched, actual
3. under the surface, hidden
4. give a concrete or actual form to
5. aversion, dislike, reluctance
6. original, earliest formed
7. to pacify, to tranquilize
8. heroic act, deed of renown
9. dark complexion
10. challenged, provoked to combat
11. domineering, arrogant
12. beseech, pray for earnestly
13. immature, unsophisticated
14. difficult to deal with
15. fearfully, suspiciously
16. clearly in view, distinguishable

A=	B=	C=	D=
E=	F=	G=	H=
I=	J=	K=	L=
M=	N=	O=	P=

The Call of the Wild Vocabulary Magic Squares 4 Answer Key

Match the definition with the vocabulary word. Put your answers in the magic squares below. When your answers are correct, all columns and rows will add to the same number.

A. IMPERIOUSLY
B. CALLOWNESS
C. EXPLOIT
D. TANGIBLE
E. INCARNATE
F. PRIMORDIAL
G. APPREHENSIVELY
H. SWARTHY
I. REPUGNANCE
J. LATENT
K. DEFIED
L. CONSPICUOUS
M. FORMIDABLE
N. IMPLORINGLY
O. IMPORTUNED
P. APPEASE

1. to urge repeatedly
2. something that can be touched, actual
3. under the surface, hidden
4. give a concrete or actual form to
5. aversion, dislike, reluctance
6. original, earliest formed
7. to pacify, to tranquilize
8. heroic act, deed of renown
9. dark complexion
10. challenged, provoked to combat
11. domineering, arrogant
12. beseech, pray for earnestly
13. immature, unsophisticated
14. difficult to deal with
15. fearfully, suspiciously
16. clearly in view, distinguishable

A=11	B=13	C=8	D=2
E=4	F=6	G=15	H=9
I=5	J=3	K=10	L=16
M=14	N=12	O=1	P=7

The Call of the Wild Vocabulary Word Search 1

Words are placed backwards, forward, diagonally, up and down. Clues listed below can help you find the words. Circle the hidden vocabulary words in the maze.

```
C R E M N A N T S L T A N G I B L E P P
O M S D O D Z N N F R B B B N Y P R R H
N Y W E I A K H E P E W Q T C D R E I B
S K A F T U Y D J C V J X R A H O T M P
P L R I A N Q F S U O I C A R O V A O D
I W T E L T X U E V C D I N N R O L R T
C S H D E E X T L Y E N M S A E C I D T
U G Y C V D Q I B S Q I P I T P A A I N
O L A T E N T L A J X M L E E U T T A Q
U P L N R R R E D W N P O N Q G I E L X
S A M S T C P L I Q X E R T L N O D P M
M L Z B F P X Y M J B R I M G A N H S C
P P A H A X S D R C Y I N W J N P B A D
S I P S Q Y J J O E H O G D K C X L E S
C T B Y S X M T F R J U L D W E L N N C
B A N H A A H T C T R S Y Q B O U T N B
H N G X R Q I O T I W L E M W T V R Q K
S T M K D F P L M T T Y D N R D S C H M
K X Z F U I R Y E U S V E O B X Z Q R B
E X P L O I T I N D I S P E N S A B L E
K T N U U V W L N E S M M M W L D X M V
V V S N S R E A L M I R I A S P I R E D
```

a region (5)
a scrap, fragment, remaining (7)
abundant (7)
apt, clever (4)
astonishing disclosure (10)
attacked, assaulted (8)
aversion, dislike, reluctance (10)
beseech, pray for earnestly (11)
challenged, provoked to combat (6)
clearly in view, distinguishable (11)
dark complexion (7)
difficult to deal with (10)
difficult, laborious (7)
discouraged, intimidated (7)
domineering, arrogant (11)
fleeting, momentary (9)
give a concrete or actual form to (9)
heroic act, deed of renown (7)
immature, unsophisticated (10)
infallible, unmistakable (9)
necessary, essential (13)

original, earliest formed (10)
ravenous (9)
secret, private (6)
serving no useful purpose (8)
something that can be touched, actual (8)
something that stimulates anger (11)
to aim at high things (7)
to hamper, obstruct (6)
to pacify, to tranquilize (7)
to take revenge, reprisal (10)
to urge repeatedly (10)
trembling or throbbing (9)
under the surface, hidden (6)

The Call of the Wild Vocabulary Word Search 1 Answer Key

Words are placed backwards, forward, diagonally, up and down. Clues listed below can help you find the words. Circle the hidden vocabulary words in the maze.

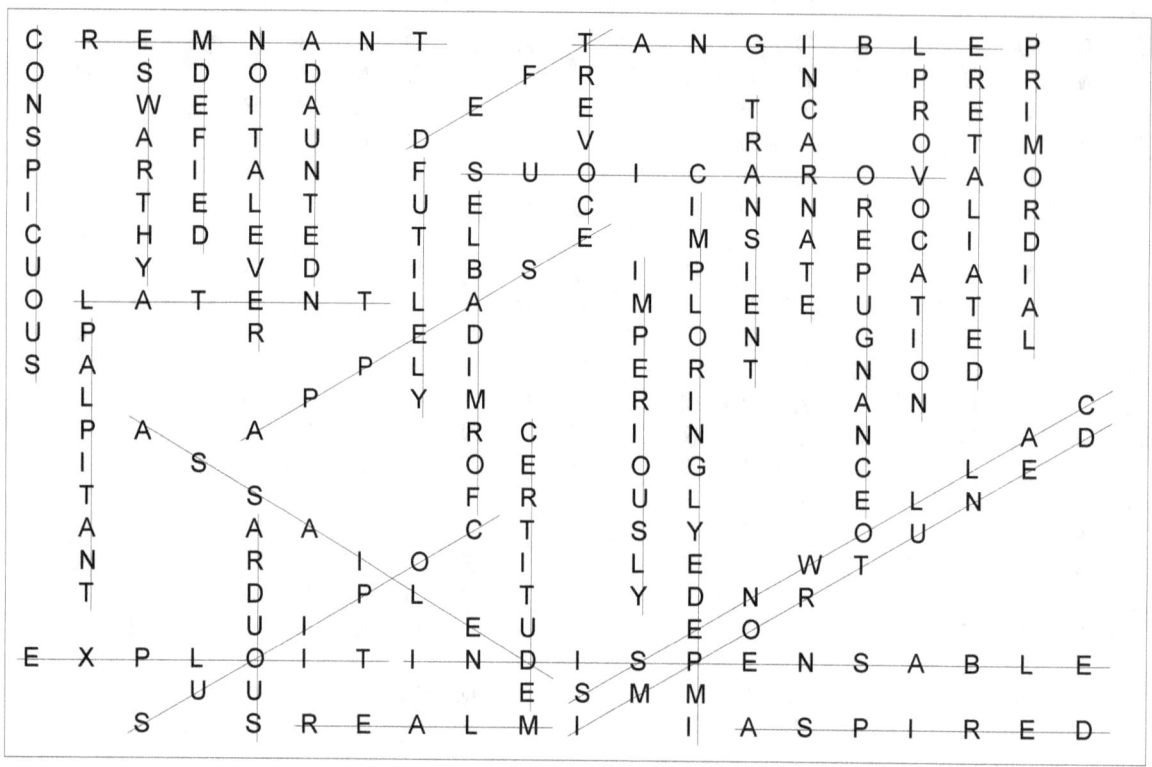

a region (5)
a scrap, fragment, remaining (7)
abundant (7)
apt, clever (4)
astonishing disclosure (10)
attacked, assaulted (8)
aversion, dislike, reluctance (10)
beseech, pray for earnestly (11)
challenged, provoked to combat (6)
clearly in view, distinguishable (11)
dark complexion (7)
difficult to deal with (10)
difficult, laborious (7)
discouraged, intimidated (7)
domineering, arrogant (11)
fleeting, momentary (9)
give a concrete or actual form to (9)
heroic act, deed of renown (7)
immature, unsophisticated (10)
infallible, unmistakable (9)
necessary, essential (13)

original, earliest formed (10)
ravenous (9)
secret, private (6)
serving no useful purpose (8)
something that can be touched, actual (8)
something that stimulates anger (11)
to aim at high things (7)
to hamper, obstruct (6)
to pacify, to tranquilize (7)
to take revenge, reprisal (10)
to urge repeatedly (10)
trembling or throbbing (9)
under the surface, hidden (6)

The Call of the Wild Vocabulary Word Search 2

Words are placed backwards, forward, diagonally, up and down. Clues listed below can help you find the words. Circle the hidden vocabulary words in the maze.

```
P F W R M R E V E L A T I O N R Q E R Y
A P P R E H E N S I V E L Y L G T C Z P
L C D K X M X L Y P C C Z V V A Y N I K
P K E M F R N H D Y S C T O N D L A N Z
I T N E I S N A R T W T D R G K G N D J
T X U N E P G Q N Z F D A A X H N G I P
A J T P D J R M J T V C Y C F Q I U S M
N R R C U Z F I N R N C R I O C R P P V
T C O G T S G L M I D F G O R N O E E D
P O P H I S D T N O U C Z U M M L R N X
M P M V T E T R O T R P D S I B P Z S R
C I I P R N M K I D S D W V D H M T A G
S O D I E W M L T E M X I L A F I K B G
W U P T C O E C A F A T M A B O X Y L D
A S S A I L E D C T R E T A L I A T E D
A T W C Y L P R O E D M M P E P N I L K
S J K A N A J G V F U F X S P E F E B P
M L A E R C W O O W O E W E T E D D I B
C F Y G P T C C R T U G A A D E M X G J
T C K C Y V H S P G S S L G P J F B N W
D A U N T E D Y S Y W J E J R M G J M P A H
I M P E R I O U S L Y V I B M J D X T B
```

a region (5)
a scrap, fragment, remaining (7)
abundant (7)
apt, clever (4)
astonishing disclosure (10)
attacked, assaulted (8)
aversion, dislike, reluctance (10)
beseech, pray for earnestly (11)
challenged, provoked to combat (6)
dark complexion (7)
difficult to deal with (10)
difficult, laborious (7)
discouraged, intimidated (7)
domineering, arrogant (11)
fearfully, suspiciously (14)
fleeting, momentary (9)
give a concrete or actual form to (9)
heroic act, deed of renown (7)
immature, unsophisticated (10)
infallible, unmistakable (9)
necessary, essential (13)

original, earliest formed (10)
ravenous (9)
secret, private (6)
serving no useful purpose (8)
something that can be touched, actual (8)
something that stimulates anger (11)
to aim at high things (7)
to hamper, obstruct (6)
to pacify, to tranquilize (7)
to take revenge, reprisal (10)
to urge repeatedly (10)
trembling or throbbing (9)
under the surface, hidden (6)

The Call of the Wild Vocabulary Word Search 2 Answer Key

Words are placed backwards, forward, diagonally, up and down. Clues listed below can help you find the words. Circle the hidden vocabulary words in the maze.

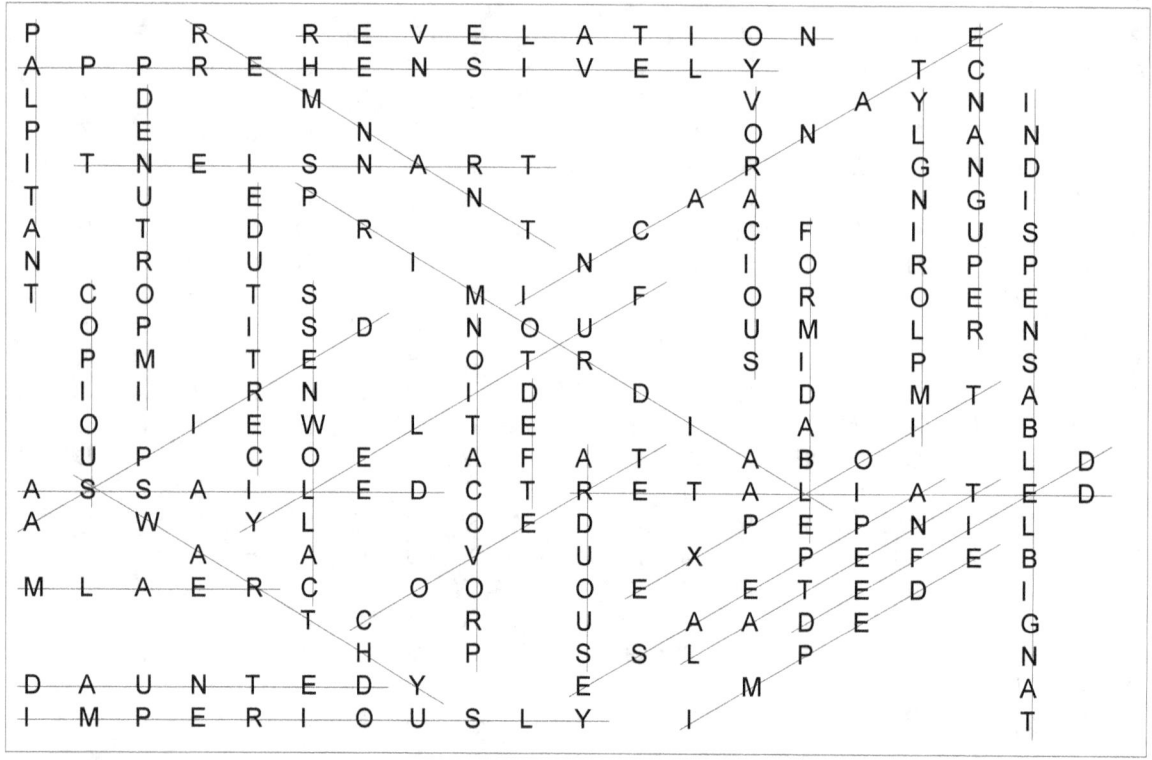

a region (5)
a scrap, fragment, remaining (7)
abundant (7)
apt, clever (4)
astonishing disclosure (10)
attacked, assaulted (8)
aversion, dislike, reluctance (10)
beseech, pray for earnestly (11)
challenged, provoked to combat (6)
dark complexion (7)
difficult to deal with (10)
difficult, laborious (7)
discouraged, intimidated (7)
domineering, arrogant (11)
fearfully, suspiciously (14)
fleeting, momentary (9)
give a concrete or actual form to (9)
heroic act, deed of renown (7)
immature, unsophisticated (10)
infallible, unmistakable (9)
necessary, essential (13)

original, earliest formed (10)
ravenous (9)
secret, private (6)
serving no useful purpose (8)
something that can be touched, actual (8)
something that stimulates anger (11)
to aim at high things (7)
to hamper, obstruct (6)
to pacify, to tranquilize (7)
to take revenge, reprisal (10)
to urge repeatedly (10)
trembling or throbbing (9)
under the surface, hidden (6)

The Call of the Wild Vocabulary Word Search 3

Words are placed backwards, forward, diagonally, up and down. Words listed below are included in the maze. Circle the hidden vocabulary words in the maze.

```
C E R T I T U D E K R E T A L I A T E D
F L T N J S V G C K T N R B Y Z C N Z P
K B W K L W S K C G A B Z L L Y O A S F
W A M P F A W H L N W T G N S L N T Z K
Z D P Y N R Y C M M Q N N N U L S I T R
S I Z H T T X E M L I M C R O T P P Z Q
H M N H K H R V C R P J A E I K I L Q Q
Y R N W P Y M C O L Z N L P R T C A Z K
Z O X L H D M L T V Q M L U E A U P L L
T F S D K J P A O Y S T O G P N O L A W
B H P P E M B R P D Z H W N M G U M I G
I R B R I F A F C P N X N A I S R D S
I M E O F C I G H F E X E N T B R Y R P
N Y P V I N B E E C J A S C D L L Y O S
C A T O E J A R D U O U S E R E A L M W
A S U C R L L S E A F V F E L C F R I D
R S J A M T A K P Z U N E I D O P T R W
N A L T B N U T M I S N T R B P T Y P Y
A I V I C E T N I N R U T Q T I C J J C
T L H O K T V M E O F E L E J O V C H Y
E E N N W A L F Y D N N D Y D U R Z W S
Y D E X P L O I T P M T R A N S I E N T
```

APPEASE	DAUNTED	IMPORTUNED	RETALIATED
ARDUOUS	DEFIED	INCARNATE	REVELATION
ASPIRED	DEFT	LATENT	SWARTHY
ASSAILED	EXPLOIT	PALPITANT	TANGIBLE
CALLOWNESS	FORMIDABLE	PRIMORDIAL	TRANSIENT
CERTITUDE	FUTILELY	PROVOCATION	VORACIOUS
CONSPICUOUS	IMPEDE	REALM	
COPIOUS	IMPERIOUSLY	REMNANT	
COVERT	IMPLORINGLY	REPUGNANCE	

The Call of the Wild Vocabulary Word Search 3 Answer Key

Words are placed backwards, forward, diagonally, up and down. Words listed below are included in the maze. Circle the hidden vocabulary words in the maze.

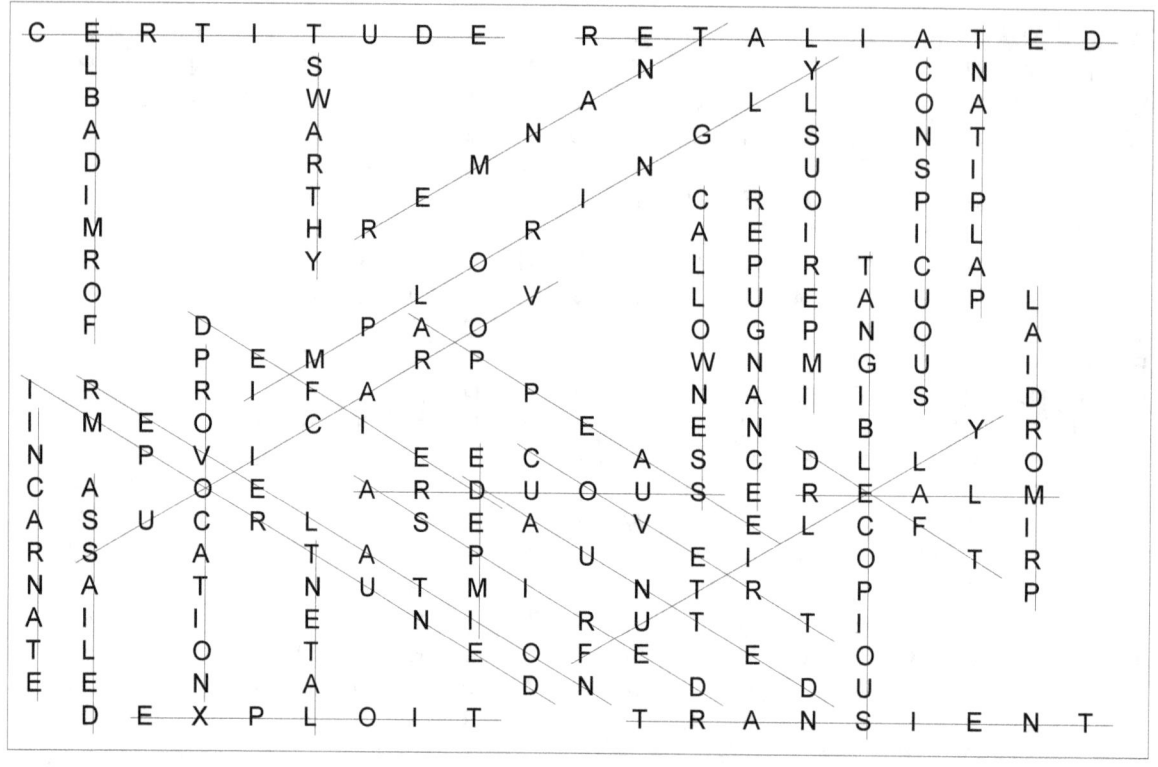

APPEASE	DAUNTED	IMPORTUNED	RETALIATED
ARDUOUS	DEFIED	INCARNATE	REVELATION
ASPIRED	DEFT	LATENT	SWARTHY
ASSAILED	EXPLOIT	PALPITANT	TANGIBLE
CALLOWNESS	FORMIDABLE	PRIMORDIAL	TRANSIENT
CERTITUDE	FUTILELY	PROVOCATION	VORACIOUS
CONSPICUOUS	IMPEDE	REALM	
COPIOUS	IMPERIOUSLY	REMNANT	
COVERT	IMPLORINGLY	REPUGNANCE	

The Call of the Wild Vocabulary Word Search 4

Words are placed backwards, forward, diagonally, up and down. Words listed below are included in the maze. Circle the hidden vocabulary words in the maze.

```
P R I M O R D I A L V O R A C I O U S L
R Y T I N D I S P E N S A B L E F N J K
E L R P D T N V Q H G M J F M R S V P M
P T A J S U O U C I P S N O C W H Y R M
U M N Y L E V I S N E H E R P P A R O T
G D S L H G H N H F G D N M B A R A V X
N H I I L L X C C D T Y N I S L R S O Q
A G E M K X Y A Z X Q L D D W P E S C G
N W N P V J K R Y Z C G T A A I M A A L
C K T O Z Z M N M V M N A B R T N I T J
E Y S R D D S A B L C I N L T A A L I L
P L F T T S D T A F A R G E H N N E O N
A R D U O U S E X P L O I T Y T T D N V
W B E N T W R K F A L L B M T N E A O M
R S F E R I S N T T O P L F P R Q U I S
K J I D R U L E G P W M E S I E R N T W
T R E V O C N E J G N I P P B B D T A B
D P D I V T G D L X E W S P G W F E L Z
B H P T F W V V K Y S A S F P R X D E Z
K O L S N G P B W P S N P W W D J Q V J
C R E T A L I A T E D U T I T R E C E Z
I M P E R I O U S L Y A P P E A S E R J
```

APPEASE	DEFT	PRIMORDIAL
APPREHENSIVELY	EXPLOIT	PROVOCATION
ARDUOUS	FORMIDABLE	REALM
ASPIRED	FUTILELY	REMNANT
ASSAILED	IMPEDE	REPUGNANCE
CALLOWNESS	IMPERIOUSLY	RETALIATED
CERTITUDE	IMPLORINGLY	REVELATION
CONSPICUOUS	IMPORTUNED	SWARTHY
COPIOUS	INCARNATE	TANGIBLE
COVERT	INDISPENSABLE	TRANSIENT
DAUNTED	LATENT	VORACIOUS
DEFIED	PALPITANT	

The Call of the Wild Vocabulary Word Search 4 Answer Key

Words are placed backwards, forward, diagonally, up and down. Words listed below are included in the maze. Circle the hidden vocabulary words in the maze.

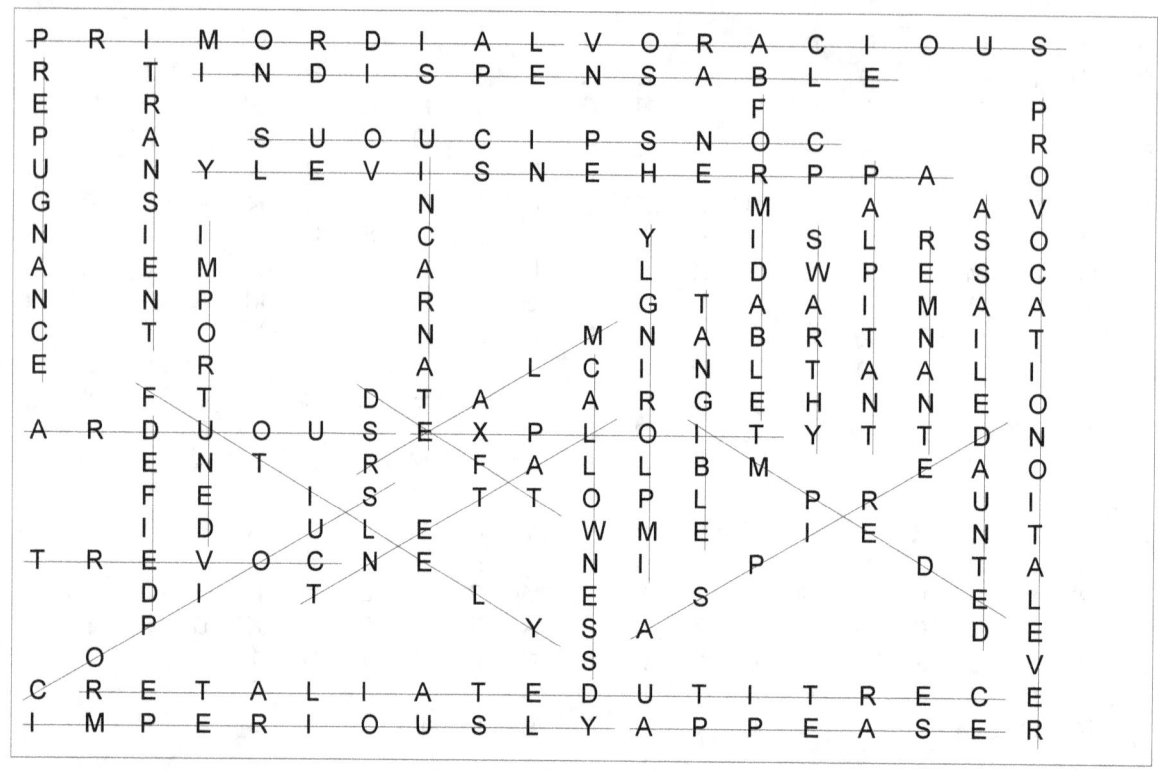

APPEASE	DEFT	PRIMORDIAL
APPREHENSIVELY	EXPLOIT	PROVOCATION
ARDUOUS	FORMIDABLE	REALM
ASPIRED	FUTILELY	REMNANT
ASSAILED	IMPEDE	REPUGNANCE
CALLOWNESS	IMPERIOUSLY	RETALIATED
CERTITUDE	IMPLORINGLY	REVELATION
CONSPICUOUS	IMPORTUNED	SWARTHY
COPIOUS	INCARNATE	TANGIBLE
COVERT	INDISPENSABLE	TRANSIENT
DAUNTED	LATENT	VORACIOUS
DEFIED	PALPITANT	

The Call of the Wild Vocabulary Crossword 1

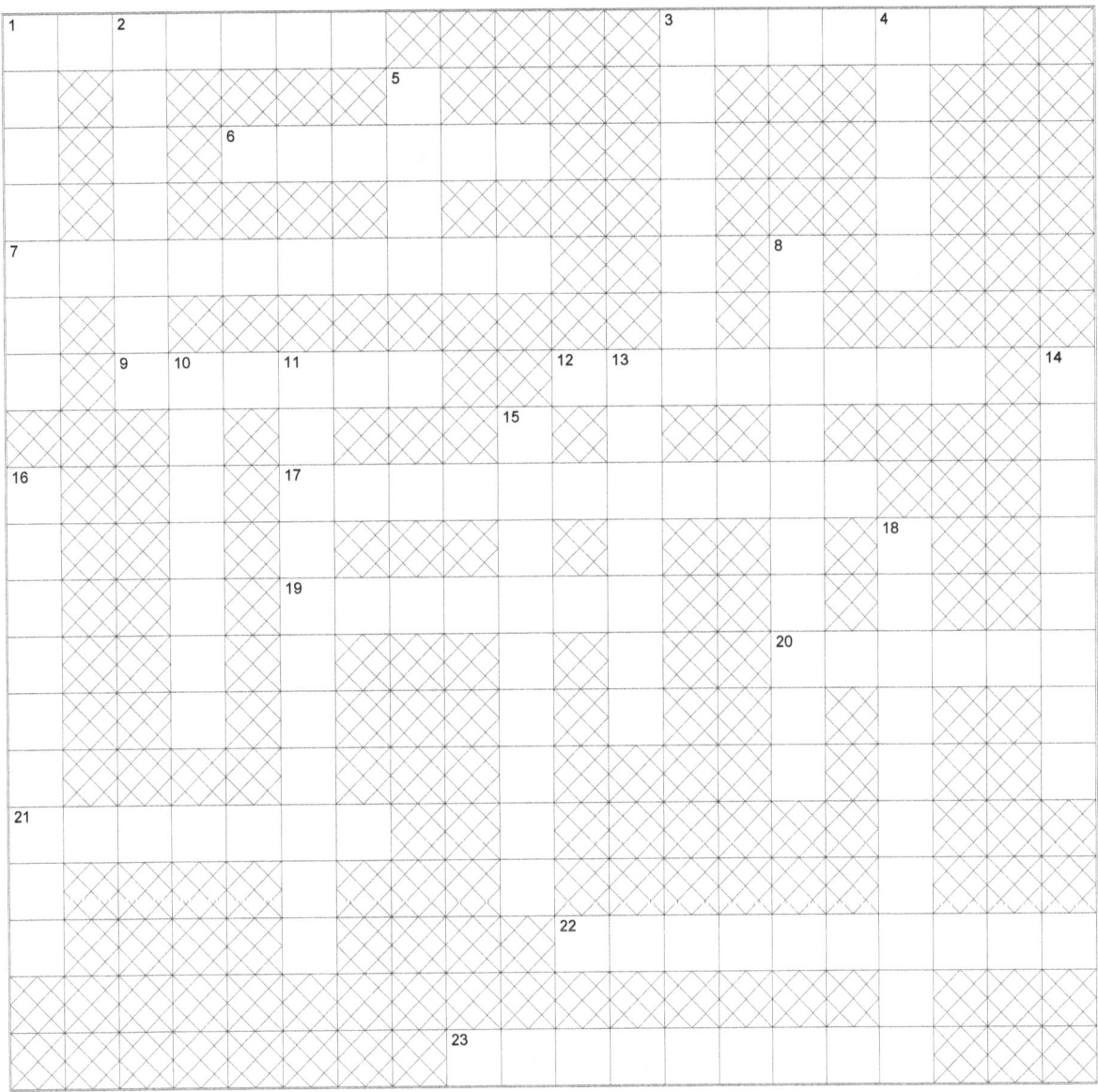

Across
1. difficult, laborious
3. secret, private
6. under the surface, hidden
7. to take revenge, reprisal
9. challenged, provoked to combat
12. attacked, assaulted
17. something that stimulates anger
19. a scrap, fragment, remaining
20. to hamper, obstruct
21. to pacify, to tranquilize
22. immature, unsophisticated
23. infallible, unmistakable

Down
1. to aim at high things
2. discouraged, intimidated
3. abundant
4. a region
5. apt, clever
8. original, earliest formed
10. heroic act, deed of renown
11. domineering, arrogant
13. dark complexion
14. serving no useful purpose
15. ravenous
16. trembling or throbbing
18. aversion, dislike, reluctance

The Call of the Wild Vocabulary Crossword 1 Answer Key

Across
1. difficult, laborious
3. secret, private
6. under the surface, hidden
7. to take revenge, reprisal
9. challenged, provoked to combat
12. attacked, assaulted
17. something that stimulates anger
19. a scrap, fragment, remaining
20. to hamper, obstruct
21. to pacify, to tranquilize
22. immature, unsophisticated
23. infallible, unmistakable

Down
1. to aim at high things
2. discouraged, intimidated
3. abundant
4. a region
5. apt, clever
8. original, earliest formed
10. heroic act, deed of renown
11. domineering, arrogant
13. dark complexion
14. serving no useful purpose
15. ravenous
16. trembling or throbbing
18. aversion, dislike, reluctance

The Call of the Wild Vocabulary Crossword 2

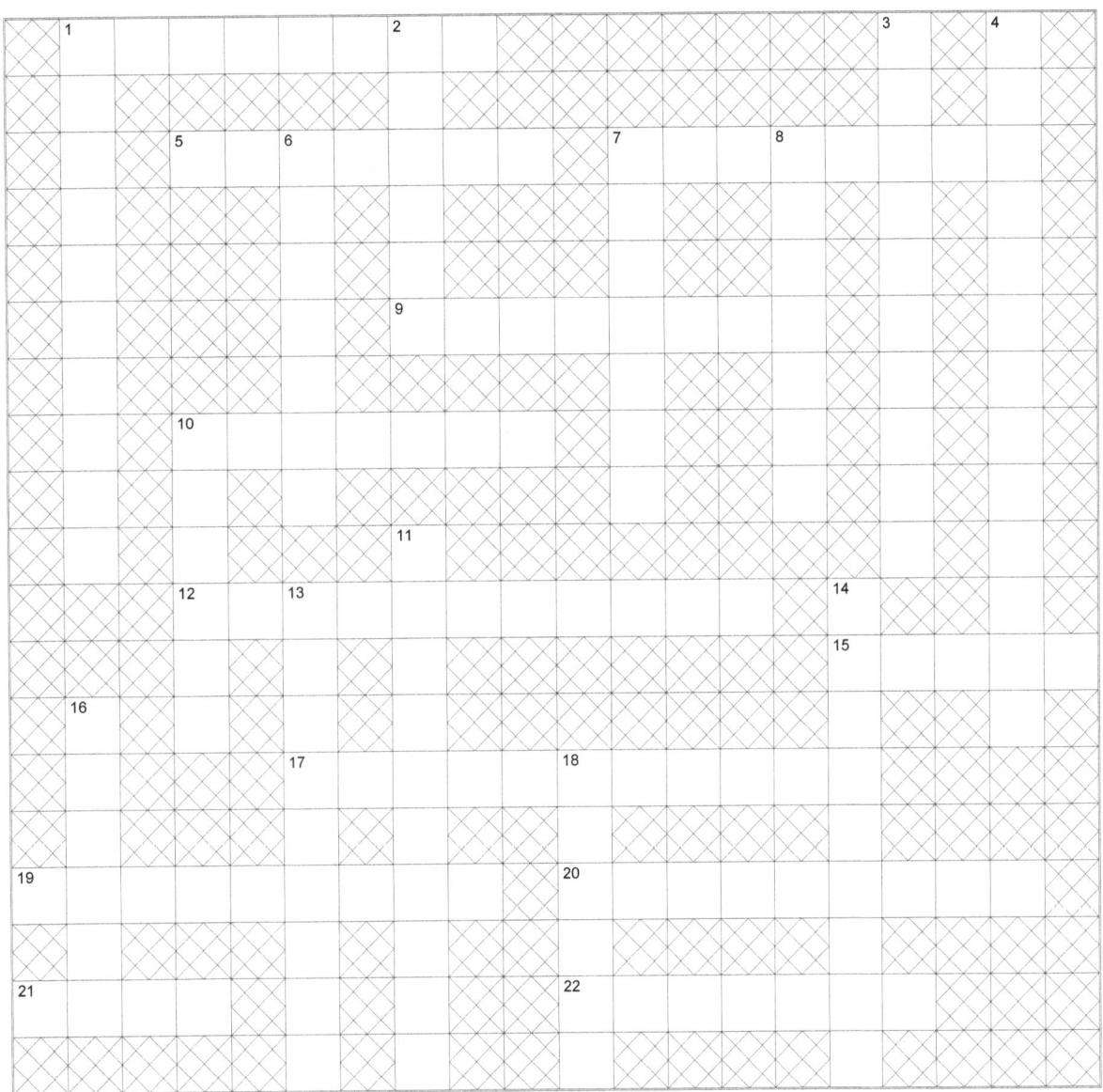

Across
1. serving no useful purpose
5. dark complexion
7. attacked, assaulted
9. something that can be touched, actual
10. discouraged, intimidated
12. domineering, arrogant
15. a region
17. something that stimulates anger
19. infallible, unmistakable
20. ravenous
21. apt, clever
22. a scrap, fragment, remaining

Down
1. difficult to deal with
2. under the surface, hidden
3. immature, unsophisticated
4. necessary, essential
6. difficult, laborious
7. to aim at high things
8. to pacify, to tranquilize
10. challenged, provoked to combat
11. original, earliest formed
13. trembling or throbbing
14. fleeting, momentary
16. to hamper, obstruct
18. secret, private

The Call of the Wild Vocabulary Crossword 2 Answer Key

Across
1. serving no useful purpose
5. dark complexion
7. attacked, assaulted
9. something that can be touched, actual
10. discouraged, intimidated
12. domineering, arrogant
15. a region
17. something that stimulates anger
19. infallible, unmistakable
20. ravenous
21. apt, clever
22. a scrap, fragment, remaining

Down
1. difficult to deal with
2. under the surface, hidden
3. immature, unsophisticated
4. necessary, essential
6. difficult, laborious
7. to aim at high things
8. to pacify, to tranquilize
10. challenged, provoked to combat
11. original, earliest formed
13. trembling or throbbing
14. fleeting, momentary
16. to hamper, obstruct
18. secret, private

The Call of the Wild Vocabulary Crossword 3

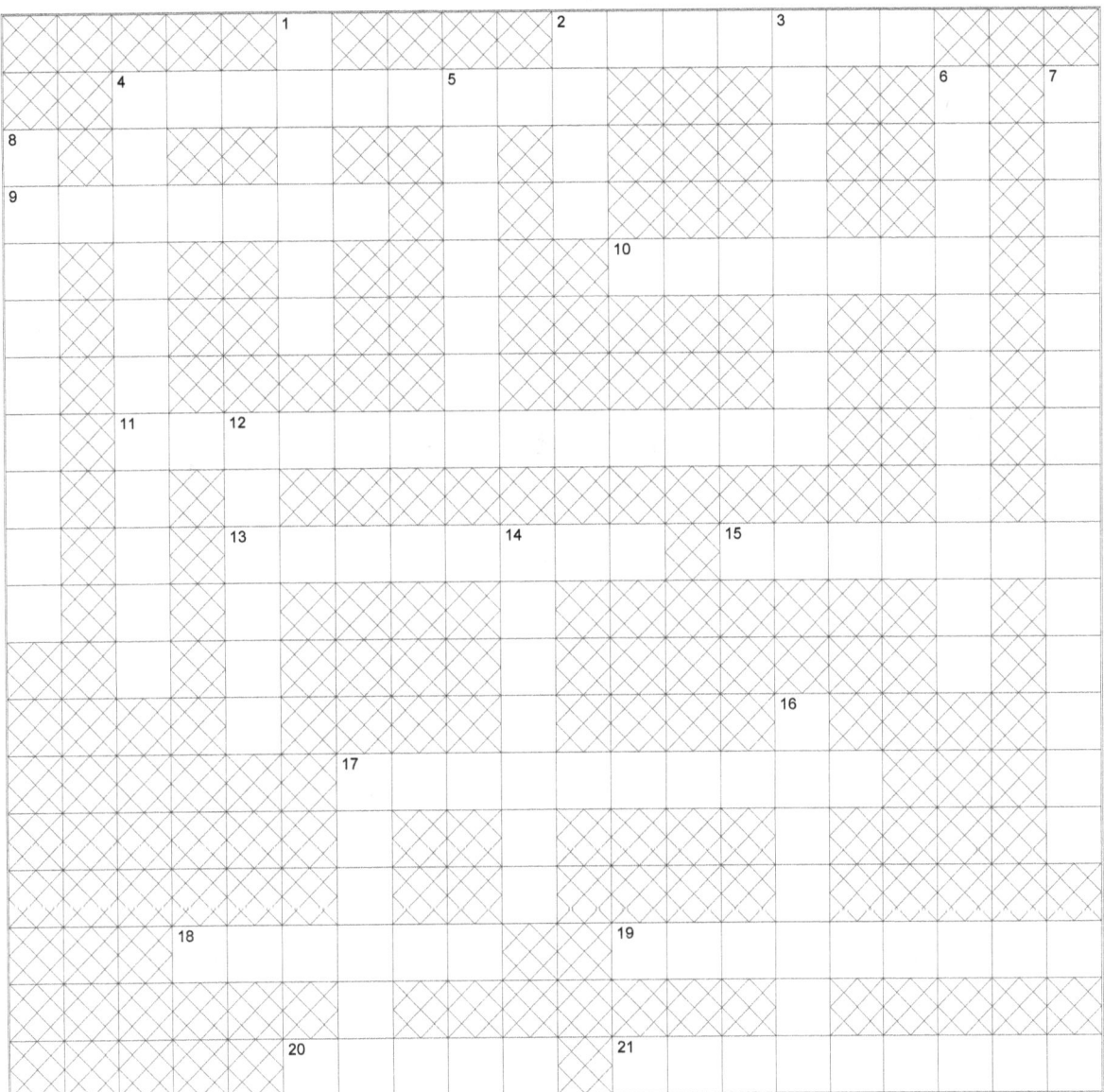

Across
2. discouraged, intimidated
4. give a concrete or actual form to
9. to aim at high things
10. abundant
11. necessary, essential
13. serving no useful purpose
15. difficult, laborious
17. to urge repeatedly
18. secret, private
19. ravenous
20. a region
21. infallible, unmistakable

Down
1. under the surface, hidden
2. apt, clever
3. something that can be touched, actual
4. beseech, pray for earnestly
5. to pacify, to tranquilize
6. clearly in view, distinguishable
7. fearfully, suspiciously
8. trembling or throbbing
12. challenged, provoked to combat
14. heroic act, deed of renown
16. a scrap, fragment, remaining
17. to hamper, obstruct

The Call of the Wild Vocabulary Crossword 3 Answer Key

Across
2. discouraged, intimidated
4. give a concrete or actual form to
9. to aim at high things
10. abundant
11. necessary, essential
13. serving no useful purpose
15. difficult, laborious
17. to urge repeatedly
18. secret, private
19. ravenous
20. a region
21. infallible, unmistakable

Down
1. under the surface, hidden
2. apt, clever
3. something that can be touched, actual
4. beseech, pray for earnestly
5. to pacify, to tranquilize
6. clearly in view, distinguishable
7. fearfully, suspiciously
8. trembling or throbbing
12. challenged, provoked to combat
14. heroic act, deed of renown
16. a scrap, fragment, remaining
17. to hamper, obstruct

Answers filled in the grid:

Across:
2. DAUNTED
4. INCARNATE
9. ASPIRED
10. COPIOUS
11. INDISPENSABLE
13. FUTILELY
15. ARDUOUS
17. IMPORTUNED
18. COVERT
19. VORACIOUS
20. REALM
21. CERTITUDE

Down:
1. LATENT (spelled down: L-A-P-L-P-I-T-A-N-T... actual: palpitant column — verify)
2. DEFT
3. TANGIBLE
4. IMPLORED
5. APPEASE
6. CONSPICUOUS
7. APPREHENSIVELY
8. PALPITANT
12. DEFIED
14. EXPLOIT
16. REMNANT
17. IMPEDIMENT

The Call of the Wild Vocabulary Crossword 4

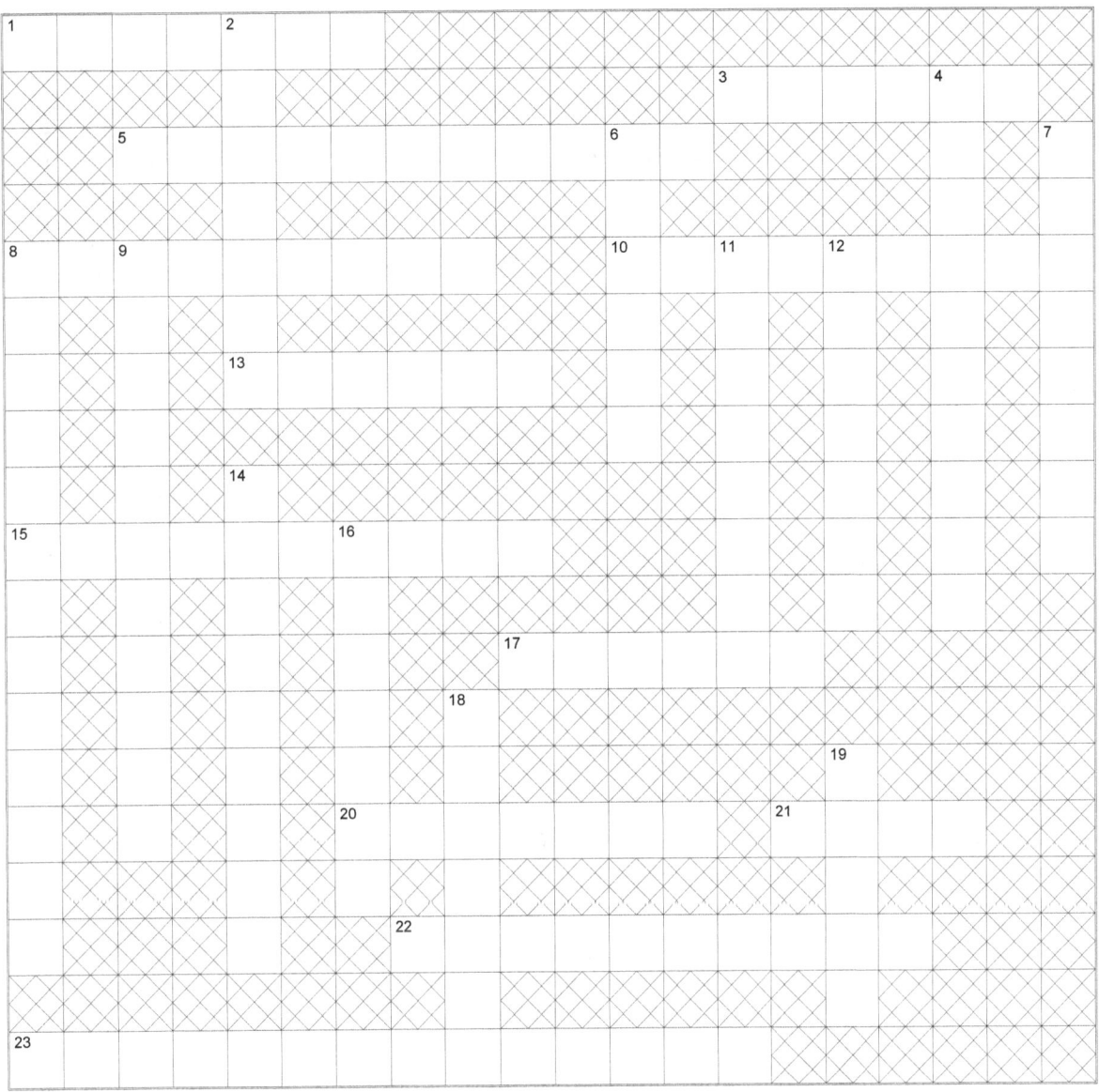

Across
1. a scrap, fragment, remaining
3. secret, private
5. beseech, pray for earnestly
8. give a concrete or actual form to
10. fleeting, momentary
13. challenged, provoked to combat
15. original, earliest formed
17. to hamper, obstruct
20. heroic act, deed of renown
21. apt, clever
22. difficult to deal with
23. fearfully, suspiciously

Down
2. to aim at high things
4. astonishing disclosure
6. under the surface, hidden
7. serving no useful purpose
8. necessary, essential
9. clearly in view, distinguishable
11. attacked, assaulted
12. dark complexion
14. ravenous
16. discouraged, intimidated
18. abundant
19. a region

The Call of the Wild Vocabulary Crossword 4 Answer Key

Across
1. a scrap, fragment, remaining
3. secret, private
5. beseech, pray for earnestly
8. give a concrete or actual form to
10. fleeting, momentary
13. challenged, provoked to combat
15. original, earliest formed
17. to hamper, obstruct
20. heroic act, deed of renown
21. apt, clever
22. difficult to deal with
23. fearfully, suspiciously

Down
2. to aim at high things
4. astonishing disclosure
6. under the surface, hidden
7. serving no useful purpose
8. necessary, essential
9. clearly in view, distinguishable
11. attacked, assaulted
12. dark complexion
14. ravenous
16. discouraged, intimidated
18. abundant
19. a region

The Call of the Wild Vocabulary Juggle Letters 1

1. AUETDDN = 1. _____
   discouraged, intimidated

2. NTLAEGBI = 2. _____
   something that can be touched, actual

3. DNROPTMEUI = 3. _____
   to urge repeatedly

4. PDERSAI = 4. _____
   to aim at high things

5. YLMLOPRIIGN = 5. _____
   beseech, pray for earnestly

6. POCIUOS = 6. _____
   abundant

7. APPESAE = 7. _____
   to pacify, to tranquilize

8. IFUEYLTL = 8. _____
   serving no useful purpose

9. IATLANTPP = 9. _____
   trembling or throbbing

10. POELXIT =10. _____
    heroic act, deed of renown

11. RIDAIPLMRO =11. _____
    original, earliest formed

12. FEDT =12. _____
    apt, clever

13. IRATSENTN =13. _____
    fleeting, momentary

14. ADBILSSIENENP =14. _____
    necessary, essential

15. UOARSUD =15. _____
    difficult, laborious

The Call of the Wild Vocabulary Juggle Letters 1 Answer Key

1. AUETDDN = 1. DAUNTED
   discouraged, intimidated

2. NTLAEGBI = 2. TANGIBLE
   something that can be touched, actual

3. DNROPTMEUI = 3. IMPORTUNED
   to urge repeatedly

4. PDERSAI = 4. ASPIRED
   to aim at high things

5. YLMLOPRIIGN = 5. IMPLORINGLY
   beseech, pray for earnestly

6. POCIUOS = 6. COPIOUS
   abundant

7. APPESAE = 7. APPEASE
   to pacify, to tranquilize

8. IFUEYLTL = 8. FUTILELY
   serving no useful purpose

9. IATLANTPP = 9. PALPITANT
   trembling or throbbing

10. POELXIT = 10. EXPLOIT
    heroic act, deed of renown

11. RIDAIPLMRO = 11. PRIMORDIAL
    original, earliest formed

12. FEDT = 12. DEFT
    apt, clever

13. IRATSENTN = 13. TRANSIENT
    fleeting, momentary

14. ADBILSSIENENP = 14. INDISPENSABLE
    necessary, essential

15. UOARSUD = 15. ARDUOUS
    difficult, laborious

The Call of the Wild Vocabulary Juggle Letters 2

1. ATNAICRNE = 1. _____
   give a concrete or actual form to

2. LMEAR = 2. _____
   a region

3. CSOUUPSICNO = 3. _____
   clearly in view, distinguishable

4. BSANDLINPSEIE = 4. _____
   necessary, essential

5. GNBATIEL = 5. _____
   something that can be touched, actual

6. AETNNITRS = 6. _____
   fleeting, momentary

7. TFDE = 7. _____
   apt, clever

8. YGPLONIMRIL = 8. _____
   beseech, pray for earnestly

9. TNETAL = 9. _____
   under the surface, hidden

10. IFMADLOBER = 10. _____
    difficult to deal with

11. OAOITNOCPRV = 11. _____
    something that stimulates anger

12. ELTDIEAATR = 12. _____
    to take revenge, reprisal

13. LCSSWOANEL = 13. _____
    immature, unsophisticated

14. EUIYTLFL = 14. _____
    serving no useful purpose

15. YSTHRAW = 15. _____
    dark complexion

The Call of the Wild Vocabulary Juggle Letters 2 Answer Key

1. ATNAICRNE = 1. INCARNATE
   give a concrete or actual form to

2. LMEAR = 2. REALM
   a region

3. CSOUUPSICNO = 3. CONSPICUOUS
   clearly in view, distinguishable

4. BSANDLINPSEIE = 4. INDISPENSABLE
   necessary, essential

5. GNBATIEL = 5. TANGIBLE
   something that can be touched, actual

6. AETNNITRS = 6. TRANSIENT
   fleeting, momentary

7. TFDE = 7. DEFT
   apt, clever

8. YGPLONIMRIL = 8. IMPLORINGLY
   beseech, pray for earnestly

9. TNETAL = 9. LATENT
   under the surface, hidden

10. IFMADLOBER = 10. FORMIDABLE
    difficult to deal with

11. OAOITNOCPRV = 11. PROVOCATION
    something that stimulates anger

12. ELTDIEAATR = 12. RETALIATED
    to take revenge, reprisal

13. LCSSWOANEL = 13. CALLOWNESS
    immature, unsophisticated

14. EUIYTLFL = 14. FUTILELY
    serving no useful purpose

15. YSTHRAW = 15. SWARTHY
    dark complexion

The Call of the Wild Vocabulary Juggle Letters 3

1. CNNGEAEUPR = 1. _____
   aversion, dislike, reluctance

2. ELRAM = 2. _____
   a region

3. SDRIEPA = 3. _____
   to aim at high things

4. LIORGPMLYIN = 4. _____
   beseech, pray for earnestly

5. ERVOCT = 5. _____
   secret, private

6. EDEIDF = 6. _____
   challenged, provoked to combat

7. LETNTA = 7. _____
   under the surface, hidden

8. NITOACRPVOO = 8. _____
   something that stimulates anger

9. VELTIANREO = 9. _____
   astonishing disclosure

10. PIOCSUNOUSC = 10. _____
    clearly in view, distinguishable

11. OXLPTEI = 11. _____
    heroic act, deed of renown

12. NEOIRUDPMT = 12. _____
    to urge repeatedly

13. NMTRAEN = 13. _____
    a scrap, fragment, remaining

14. LAVREYPEEPSHNI = 14. _____
    fearfully, suspiciously

15. LTINAPPTA = 15. _____
    trembling or throbbing

The Call of the Wild Vocabulary Juggle Letters 3 Answer Key

1. CNNGEAEUPR = 1. REPUGNANCE
   aversion, dislike, reluctance

2. ELRAM = 2. REALM
   a region

3. SDRIEPA = 3. ASPIRED
   to aim at high things

4. LIORGPMLYIN = 4. IMPLORINGLY
   beseech, pray for earnestly

5. ERVOCT = 5. COVERT
   secret, private

6. EDEIDF = 6. DEFIED
   challenged, provoked to combat

7. LETNTA = 7. LATENT
   under the surface, hidden

8. NITOACRPVOO = 8. PROVOCATION
   something that stimulates anger

9. VELTIANREO = 9. REVELATION
   astonishing disclosure

10. PIOCSUNOUSC = 10. CONSPICUOUS
    clearly in view, distinguishable

11. OXLPTEI = 11. EXPLOIT
    heroic act, deed of renown

12. NEOIRUDPMT = 12. IMPORTUNED
    to urge repeatedly

13. NMTRAEN = 13. REMNANT
    a scrap, fragment, remaining

14. LAVREYPEEPSHNI = 14. APPREHENSIVELY
    fearfully, suspiciously

15. LTINAPPTA = 15. PALPITANT
    trembling or throbbing

The Call of the Wild Vocabulary Juggle Letters 4

1. ANTMREN = 1. _____
   a scrap, fragment, remaining

2. HRWATYS = 2. _____
   dark complexion

3. TEDANDU = 3. _____
   discouraged, intimidated

4. RNGMLYILOIP = 4. _____
   beseech, pray for earnestly

5. CAISORVOU = 5. _____
   ravenous

6. ESSAAIDL = 6. _____
   attacked, assaulted

7. PUOERSYILIM = 7. _____
   domineering, arrogant

8. ELBTIGNA = 8. _____
   something that can be touched, actual

9. LEAISIDSNEBPN = 9. _____
   necessary, essential

10. ILTADETAER =10. _____
    to take revenge, reprisal

11. TNARSENIT =11. _____
    fleeting, momentary

12. EORTCV =12. _____
    secret, private

13. PEXITOL =13. _____
    heroic act, deed of renown

14. HVIYLAESEENPRP =14. _____
    fearfully, suspiciously

15. ATLETN =15. _____
    under the surface, hidden

The Call of the Wild Vocabulary Juggle Letters 4 Answer Key

1. ANTMREN = 1. REMNANT
   a scrap, fragment, remaining

2. HRWATYS = 2. SWARTHY
   dark complexion

3. TEDANDU = 3. DAUNTED
   discouraged, intimidated

4. RNGMLYILOIP = 4. IMPLORINGLY
   beseech, pray for earnestly

5. CAISORVOU = 5. VORACIOUS
   ravenous

6. ESSAAIDL = 6. ASSAILED
   attacked, assaulted

7. PUOERSYILIM = 7. IMPERIOUSLY
   domineering, arrogant

8. ELBTIGNA = 8. TANGIBLE
   something that can be touched, actual

9. LEAISIDSNEBPN = 9. INDISPENSABLE
   necessary, essential

10. ILTADETAER = 10. RETALIATED
    to take revenge, reprisal

11. TNARSENIT = 11. TRANSIENT
    fleeting, momentary

12. EORTCV = 12. COVERT
    secret, private

13. PEXITOL = 13. EXPLOIT
    heroic act, deed of renown

14. HVIYLAESEENPRP = 14. APPREHENSIVELY
    fearfully, suspiciously

15. ATLETN = 15. LATENT
    under the surface, hidden

APPEASE	to pacify, to tranquilize
APPREHENSIVELY	fearfully, suspiciously
ARDUOUS	difficult, laborious
ASPIRED	to aim at high things
ASSAILED	attacked, assaulted
CALLOWNESS	immature, unsophisticated

CERTITUDE	infallible, unmistakable
CONSPICUOUS	clearly in view, distinguishable
COPIOUS	abundant
COVERT	secret, private
DAUNTED	discouraged, intimidated
DEFIED	challenged, provoked to combat

DEFT	apt, clever
EXPLOIT	heroic act, deed of renown
FORMIDABLE	difficult to deal with
FUTILELY	serving no useful purpose
IMPEDE	to hamper, obstruct
IMPERIOUSLY	domineering, arrogant

IMPLORINGLY	beseech, pray for earnestly
IMPORTUNED	to urge repeatedly
INCARNATE	give a concrete or actual form to
INDISPENSABLE	necessary, essential
LATENT	under the surface, hidden
PALPITANT	trembling or throbbing

PRIMORDIAL	original, earliest formed
PROVOCATION	something that stimulates anger
REALM	a region
REMNANT	a scrap, fragment, remaining
REPUGNANCE	aversion, dislike, reluctance
RETALIATED	to take revenge, reprisal

REVELATION	astonishing disclosure
SWARTHY	dark complexion
TANGIBLE	something that can be touched, actual
TRANSIENT	fleeting, momentary
VORACIOUS	ravenous

The Call of the Wild Vocab

CONSPICUOUS	DEFT	INDISPENSABLE	IMPLORINGLY	FORMIDABLE
PALPITANT	APPREHENSIVELY	CALLOWNESS	IMPERIOUSLY	COPIOUS
COVERT	APPEASE	FREE SPACE	ASPIRED	TANGIBLE
ARDUOUS	PROVOCATION	INCARNATE	LATENT	REALM
TRANSIENT	SWARTHY	CERTITUDE	REVELATION	REMNANT

The Call of the Wild Vocab

PRIMORDIAL	VORACIOUS	REPUGNANCE	IMPORTUNED	ASSAILED
IMPEDE	FUTILELY	DAUNTED	DEFIED	EXPLOIT
REMNANT	REVELATION	FREE SPACE	SWARTHY	TRANSIENT
REALM	LATENT	INCARNATE	PROVOCATION	ARDUOUS
TANGIBLE	ASPIRED	RETALIATED	APPEASE	COVERT

The Call of the Wild Vocab

PALPITANT	REALM	SWARTHY	CONSPICUOUS	LATENT
COPIOUS	REPUGNANCE	ASPIRED	PROVOCATION	APPREHENSIVELY
EXPLOIT	IMPORTUNED	FREE SPACE	IMPLORINGLY	DAUNTED
COVERT	FUTILELY	RETALIATED	ARDUOUS	DEFIED
REMNANT	IMPERIOUSLY	REVELATION	CERTITUDE	DEFT

The Call of the Wild Vocab

CALLOWNESS	TRANSIENT	APPEASE	TANGIBLE	PRIMORDIAL
IMPEDE	INDISPENSABLE	VORACIOUS	ASSAILED	FORMIDABLE
DEFT	CERTITUDE	FREE SPACE	IMPERIOUSLY	REMNANT
DEFIED	ARDUOUS	RETALIATED	FUTILELY	COVERT
DAUNTED	IMPLORINGLY	INCARNATE	IMPORTUNED	EXPLOIT

The Call of the Wild Vocab

LATENT	CONSPICUOUS	ARDUOUS	SWARTHY	ASSAILED
APPEASE	CERTITUDE	IMPORTUNED	COPIOUS	REMNANT
EXPLOIT	VORACIOUS	FREE SPACE	TRANSIENT	ASPIRED
DEFIED	COVERT	DEFT	DAUNTED	REPUGNANCE
INDISPENSABLE	REVELATION	PALPITANT	FUTILELY	RETALIATED

The Call of the Wild Vocab

IMPLORINGLY	REALM	FORMIDABLE	IMPEDE	IMPERIOUSLY
APPREHENSIVELY	PROVOCATION	INCARNATE	TANGIBLE	CALLOWNESS
RETALIATED	FUTILELY	FREE SPACE	REVELATION	INDISPENSABLE
REPUGNANCE	DAUNTED	DEFT	COVERT	DEFIED
ASPIRED	TRANSIENT	PRIMORDIAL	VORACIOUS	EXPLOIT

The Call of the Wild Vocab

EXPLOIT	DAUNTED	FORMIDABLE	IMPERIOUSLY	CONSPICUOUS
LATENT	PALPITANT	VORACIOUS	SWARTHY	REMNANT
REALM	COVERT	FREE SPACE	FUTILELY	TRANSIENT
IMPEDE	ARDUOUS	INDISPENSABLE	CERTITUDE	CALLOWNESS
PROVOCATION	IMPLORINGLY	APPEASE	ASSAILED	REPUGNANCE

The Call of the Wild Vocab

DEFT	IMPORTUNED	COPIOUS	APPREHENSIVELY	PRIMORDIAL
RETALIATED	INCARNATE	DEFIED	ASPIRED	REVELATION
REPUGNANCE	ASSAILED	FREE SPACE	IMPLORINGLY	PROVOCATION
CALLOWNESS	CERTITUDE	INDISPENSABLE	ARDUOUS	IMPEDE
TRANSIENT	FUTILELY	TANGIBLE	COVERT	REALM

The Call of the Wild Vocab

IMPEDE	IMPLORINGLY	EXPLOIT	APPEASE	PALPITANT
SWARTHY	LATENT	REMNANT	COVERT	FORMIDABLE
PROVOCATION	RETALIATED	FREE SPACE	ASPIRED	REALM
APPREHENSIVELY	CONSPICUOUS	INCARNATE	INDISPENSABLE	DEFIED
CERTITUDE	IMPORTUNED	IMPERIOUSLY	TRANSIENT	REPUGNANCE

The Call of the Wild Vocab

FUTILELY	DEFT	TANGIBLE	ARDUOUS	DAUNTED
REVELATION	CALLOWNESS	PRIMORDIAL	ASSAILED	VORACIOUS
REPUGNANCE	TRANSIENT	FREE SPACE	IMPORTUNED	CERTITUDE
DEFIED	INDISPENSABLE	INCARNATE	CONSPICUOUS	APPREHENSIVELY
REALM	ASPIRED	COPIOUS	RETALIATED	PROVOCATION

The Call of the Wild Vocab

CERTITUDE	TANGIBLE	ASSAILED	DEFIED	REVELATION
APPEASE	COVERT	REMNANT	RETALIATED	ASPIRED
FUTILELY	LATENT	FREE SPACE	IMPLORINGLY	PRIMORDIAL
EXPLOIT	IMPERIOUSLY	VORACIOUS	REALM	CALLOWNESS
IMPEDE	REPUGNANCE	IMPORTUNED	PALPITANT	FORMIDABLE

The Call of the Wild Vocab

INCARNATE	COPIOUS	INDISPENSABLE	CONSPICUOUS	APPREHENSIVELY
TRANSIENT	ARDUOUS	DAUNTED	SWARTHY	DEFT
FORMIDABLE	PALPITANT	FREE SPACE	REPUGNANCE	IMPEDE
CALLOWNESS	REALM	VORACIOUS	IMPERIOUSLY	EXPLOIT
PRIMORDIAL	IMPLORINGLY	PROVOCATION	LATENT	FUTILELY

The Call of the Wild Vocab

COVERT	ARDUOUS	DEFIED	IMPORTUNED	EXPLOIT
APPEASE	LATENT	PRIMORDIAL	CONSPICUOUS	IMPEDE
DEFT	PALPITANT	FREE SPACE	PROVOCATION	IMPERIOUSLY
TANGIBLE	REVELATION	RETALIATED	ASSAILED	DAUNTED
VORACIOUS	INDISPENSABLE	CALLOWNESS	REALM	APPREHENSIVELY

The Call of the Wild Vocab

REMNANT	TRANSIENT	FUTILELY	CERTITUDE	ASPIRED
COPIOUS	SWARTHY	INCARNATE	REPUGNANCE	IMPLORINGLY
APPREHENSIVELY	REALM	FREE SPACE	INDISPENSABLE	VORACIOUS
DAUNTED	ASSAILED	RETALIATED	REVELATION	TANGIBLE
IMPERIOUSLY	PROVOCATION	FORMIDABLE	PALPITANT	DEFT

The Call of the Wild Vocab

IMPORTUNED	VORACIOUS	EXPLOIT	REMNANT	COPIOUS
ARDUOUS	FORMIDABLE	TANGIBLE	TRANSIENT	ASSAILED
ASPIRED	LATENT	FREE SPACE	DAUNTED	REVELATION
CALLOWNESS	DEFT	CONSPICUOUS	FUTILELY	REALM
REPUGNANCE	PROVOCATION	CERTITUDE	COVERT	DEFIED

The Call of the Wild Vocab

INDISPENSABLE	INCARNATE	IMPEDE	APPREHENSIVELY	APPEASE
IMPERIOUSLY	RETALIATED	IMPLORINGLY	SWARTHY	PALPITANT
DEFIED	COVERT	FREE SPACE	PROVOCATION	REPUGNANCE
REALM	FUTILELY	CONSPICUOUS	DEFT	CALLOWNESS
REVELATION	DAUNTED	PRIMORDIAL	LATENT	ASPIRED

The Call of the Wild Vocab

REPUGNANCE	REVELATION	ASPIRED	VORACIOUS	CERTITUDE
EXPLOIT	LATENT	REALM	PROVOCATION	PALPITANT
ARDUOUS	PRIMORDIAL	FREE SPACE	FUTILELY	APPEASE
IMPEDE	RETALIATED	DEFIED	COPIOUS	IMPERIOUSLY
CONSPICUOUS	APPREHENSIVELY	COVERT	INDISPENSABLE	INCARNATE

The Call of the Wild Vocab

IMPLORINGLY	DAUNTED	DEFT	IMPORTUNED	REMNANT
SWARTHY	CALLOWNESS	TANGIBLE	ASSAILED	TRANSIENT
INCARNATE	INDISPENSABLE	FREE SPACE	APPREHENSIVELY	CONSPICUOUS
IMPERIOUSLY	COPIOUS	DEFIED	RETALIATED	IMPEDE
APPEASE	FUTILELY	FORMIDABLE	PRIMORDIAL	ARDUOUS

The Call of the Wild Vocab

INDISPENSABLE	DEFIED	VORACIOUS	REMNANT	REVELATION
LATENT	CERTITUDE	FUTILELY	ARDUOUS	ASSAILED
APPREHENSIVELY	SWARTHY	FREE SPACE	APPEASE	RETALIATED
COVERT	REPUGNANCE	IMPERIOUSLY	PALPITANT	ASPIRED
DEFT	TRANSIENT	IMPORTUNED	CALLOWNESS	REALM

The Call of the Wild Vocab

FORMIDABLE	CONSPICUOUS	IMPEDE	COPIOUS	PROVOCATION
IMPLORINGLY	DAUNTED	INCARNATE	TANGIBLE	EXPLOIT
REALM	CALLOWNESS	FREE SPACE	TRANSIENT	DEFT
ASPIRED	PALPITANT	IMPERIOUSLY	REPUGNANCE	COVERT
RETALIATED	APPEASE	PRIMORDIAL	SWARTHY	APPREHENSIVELY

The Call of the Wild Vocab

FORMIDABLE	DAUNTED	PRIMORDIAL	INCARNATE	DEFIED
APPREHENSIVELY	REVELATION	ASPIRED	REALM	ASSAILED
RETALIATED	COPIOUS	FREE SPACE	COVERT	VORACIOUS
REPUGNANCE	PALPITANT	TANGIBLE	CONSPICUOUS	IMPERIOUSLY
TRANSIENT	IMPEDE	CALLOWNESS	REMNANT	LATENT

The Call of the Wild Vocab

PROVOCATION	CERTITUDE	IMPLORINGLY	FUTILELY	EXPLOIT
SWARTHY	INDISPENSABLE	DEFT	APPEASE	ARDUOUS
LATENT	REMNANT	FREE SPACE	IMPEDE	TRANSIENT
IMPERIOUSLY	CONSPICUOUS	TANGIBLE	PALPITANT	REPUGNANCE
VORACIOUS	COVERT	IMPORTUNED	COPIOUS	RETALIATED

The Call of the Wild Vocab

CERTITUDE	CONSPICUOUS	RETALIATED	REVELATION	DEFT
FORMIDABLE	IMPORTUNED	INCARNATE	APPREHENSIVELY	ASPIRED
REALM	IMPEDE	FREE SPACE	DEFIED	LATENT
ASSAILED	PRIMORDIAL	PROVOCATION	FUTILELY	CALLOWNESS
IMPERIOUSLY	COPIOUS	DAUNTED	SWARTHY	VORACIOUS

The Call of the Wild Vocab

ARDUOUS	PALPITANT	REPUGNANCE	TANGIBLE	REMNANT
EXPLOIT	TRANSIENT	INDISPENSABLE	APPEASE	COVERT
VORACIOUS	SWARTHY	FREE SPACE	COPIOUS	IMPERIOUSLY
CALLOWNESS	FUTILELY	PROVOCATION	PRIMORDIAL	ASSAILED
LATENT	DEFIED	IMPLORINGLY	IMPEDE	REALM

The Call of the Wild Vocab

REPUGNANCE	PALPITANT	REMNANT	CONSPICUOUS	FUTILELY
SWARTHY	INCARNATE	LATENT	IMPORTUNED	APPEASE
PROVOCATION	TANGIBLE	FREE SPACE	DEFT	DAUNTED
ARDUOUS	ASSAILED	IMPEDE	FORMIDABLE	VORACIOUS
EXPLOIT	CALLOWNESS	IMPLORINGLY	IMPERIOUSLY	INDISPENSABLE

The Call of the Wild Vocab

COVERT	ASPIRED	PRIMORDIAL	REVELATION	REALM
CERTITUDE	RETALIATED	DEFIED	COPIOUS	APPREHENSIVELY
INDISPENSABLE	IMPERIOUSLY	FREE SPACE	CALLOWNESS	EXPLOIT
VORACIOUS	FORMIDABLE	IMPEDE	ASSAILED	ARDUOUS
DAUNTED	DEFT	TRANSIENT	TANGIBLE	PROVOCATION

The Call of the Wild Vocab

LATENT	INDISPENSABLE	IMPLORINGLY	APPEASE	IMPORTUNED
EXPLOIT	CALLOWNESS	INCARNATE	CONSPICUOUS	COVERT
ARDUOUS	TRANSIENT	FREE SPACE	ASSAILED	ASPIRED
APPREHENSIVELY	DAUNTED	IMPEDE	IMPERIOUSLY	COPIOUS
REALM	DEFIED	REMNANT	PALPITANT	FORMIDABLE

The Call of the Wild Vocab

REVELATION	RETALIATED	DEFT	VORACIOUS	PRIMORDIAL
SWARTHY	REPUGNANCE	CERTITUDE	TANGIBLE	FUTILELY
FORMIDABLE	PALPITANT	FREE SPACE	DEFIED	REALM
COPIOUS	IMPERIOUSLY	IMPEDE	DAUNTED	APPREHENSIVELY
ASPIRED	ASSAILED	PROVOCATION	TRANSIENT	ARDUOUS

The Call of the Wild Vocab

RETALIATED	COPIOUS	TRANSIENT	ASSAILED	ASPIRED
CONSPICUOUS	IMPLORINGLY	ARDUOUS	REALM	IMPORTUNED
LATENT	FUTILELY	FREE SPACE	INDISPENSABLE	DEFT
REMNANT	CALLOWNESS	INCARNATE	REPUGNANCE	APPREHENSIVELY
VORACIOUS	COVERT	EXPLOIT	SWARTHY	REVELATION

The Call of the Wild Vocab

IMPERIOUSLY	IMPEDE	DAUNTED	APPEASE	PRIMORDIAL
FORMIDABLE	TANGIBLE	CERTITUDE	PALPITANT	PROVOCATION
REVELATION	SWARTHY	FREE SPACE	COVERT	VORACIOUS
APPREHENSIVELY	REPUGNANCE	INCARNATE	CALLOWNESS	REMNANT
DEFT	INDISPENSABLE	DEFIED	FUTILELY	LATENT

The Call of the Wild Vocab

REVELATION	IMPORTUNED	REMNANT	PROVOCATION	RETALIATED
ASSAILED	ASPIRED	COPIOUS	APPREHENSIVELY	EXPLOIT
IMPLORINGLY	COVERT	FREE SPACE	INCARNATE	ARDUOUS
REPUGNANCE	PALPITANT	APPEASE	DEFT	LATENT
DEFIED	DAUNTED	REALM	FUTILELY	TRANSIENT

The Call of the Wild Vocab

IMPEDE	INDISPENSABLE	CALLOWNESS	FORMIDABLE	IMPERIOUSLY
CONSPICUOUS	TANGIBLE	VORACIOUS	CERTITUDE	PRIMORDIAL
TRANSIENT	FUTILELY	FREE SPACE	DAUNTED	DEFIED
LATENT	DEFT	APPEASE	PALPITANT	REPUGNANCE
ARDUOUS	INCARNATE	SWARTHY	COVERT	IMPLORINGLY

www.ingramcontent.com/pod-product-compliance
Lightning Source LLC
Chambersburg PA
CBHW081457070526
44586CB00019B/2398